The Art of Segmented Woodturning

FAITHFUL (36 inches tall).

The Art of Segmented Woodturning

A Step-by-Step Guide

Malcolm J. Tibbetts

Linden Publishing

Fresno

The Art of Segmented Woodturning

A Step-by-Step Guide

by

Malcolm J. Tibbetts

1113141210

ISBN 10: 0-941936-86-4

ISBN 13: 978-0-941936-86-6

Printed in the United States of America

Library of Congress Cataloging-in-Publication data
Tibbetts, Malcolm, 1949-
    The art of segmented woodturning : a step-by-step guide / by Malcolm Tibbetts.
    p. cm.
    Includes bibliographical references and index.
    ISBN 0-941936-86-4 (pbk. : alk.paper)
    1. Turning. 2. Woodwork. I. Title.
    TT203.T53 2004
    684'.08--dc22

2004012777

Linden Publishing Inc.
2006 S. Mary
Fresno, CA
www.lindenpub.com
800-345-4447

Dedication

for Tere
for everything

Special Thanks to:

My grand-dad "Rap," who introduced me to the joys of working with wood.

Ron Goldman for his recommendation.

Richard Sorsky for the opportunity and for his guidance.

Sandy Hogan for her invaluable help with the English language.

John Kelsey and his team for design and layout.

My fellow woodturners, especially members of the NORCAL chapter of the American Association of Woodturners, for their encouragement.

...and with the utmost appreciation, those who have rewarded me with the ultimate compliment by acquiring my work, which has allowed me to pursue this fascinating art form.

Table of Contents

PEARLS FROM THE FOREST (34 inches tall)

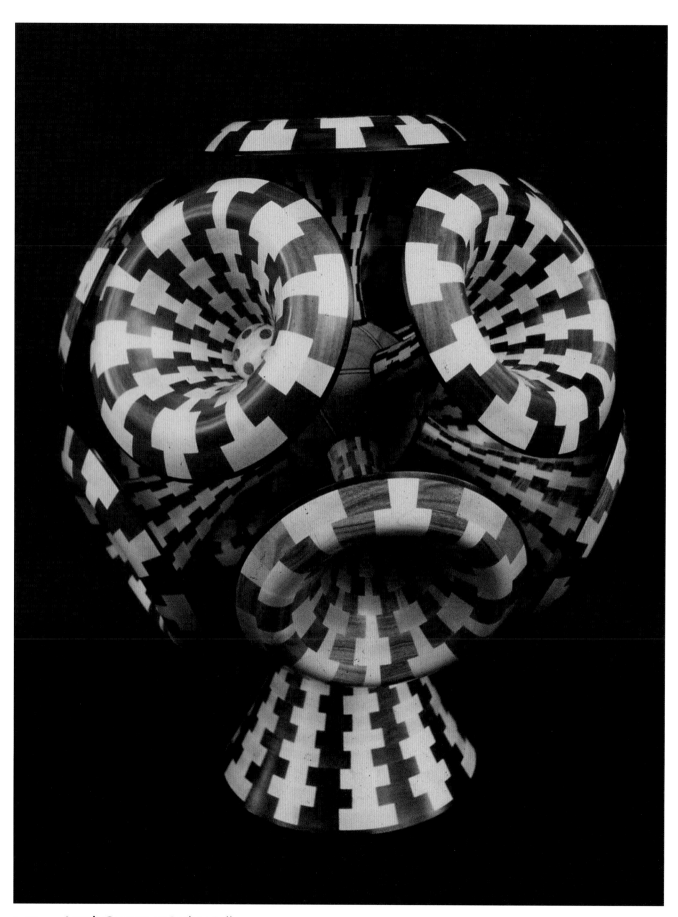

1-01　*ALICE'S GARDEN.* 35 inches tall.

1.

Introduction

From the time I built my first birdhouse at age five in my granddad's shop, I have always had a fascination with wood. More than thirty years ago, after moving into an empty house, with my wife's encouragement, I purchased a table saw instead of inexpensive, affordable furniture. Following twenty years of building furniture for our home in Lake Tahoe, I discovered the magical capabilities of the lathe. As I look back at my past furniture designs, it strikes me that I have always experimented with designs using contrasting wood color combinations. Given my prior woodworking experiences and my ownership of the necessary tools, it was only natural that I gravitated towards segmented woodturning.

Segmented woodturning, or as it has been called, polychromatic woodturning, has been around for a very long time. Many years ago someone probably had the need for a bowl that was larger than their largest piece of wood and thought, "I'll just glue two pieces together." From that moment in time, the "art" of segmented turning has continued to evolve. Long before I glued together my first ring of segments, many other woodturners pursued this art form with great success, providing inspiration to those of us that followed their lead. In the 1970s and 1980s, Emmett Brown and Cyril Brown, with their publication of *Polychromatic Assembly for Woodturning*, inspired thousands of turners to experiment. Dale Nish, in 1980, with his publication of *Artistic Woodturning*, sent a signal to the woodturning world, that it was OK to glue wood together, and woodturners continued to enthusiastically experiment. Ray Allen, Giles Gilson, Bud Latven, Lincoln Seitzman, and Mike Shuler are just a few of the very talented artists that have also inspired me. These artists opened doors for all of us, but they, like all of us, had to start with their own very first segmented project. If you are looking for a new challenge, then it is my hope that these pages will provide you with the techniques and inspiration needed to create your own first segmented turning. If you have already started down this path, then I hope some of my ideas will renew your interest and encourage you to develop new challenges.

On these pages, I have attempted to share my experiences. I have described the techniques that have worked for me and in some cases, those that have not worked. I want to make it clear, that I do not offer the methods described on these pages as the only way. I know from casual contact with other turners, that everyone develops their own way. I should also point out that not all of these techniques are my own invention. Woodturners are very sharing and many techniques have been offered to the public in workshops, symposiums, and magazine articles; I have tried to give credit where it is due.

Segmented woodturning is much more than gluing together pieces of wood into a bowl. It is about creating exciting objects that challenge you and stimulate the interest and enjoyment of others. It need not be a paint-by-the-numbers type of craft — it can be a real opportunity to express oneself with very few limitations. This activity requires extremely precise woodworking skills and often requires a little inventiveness. As a segmented turner, you are free from the boundaries of a single block of wood. You have unlimited choices regarding size, shape, and color combinations. The possibilities are endless, which is why it continues to keep my interest. ALICE'S GARDEN (photo 1-01) is a perfect example of a form that would be almost impossible to create from a single block of wood.

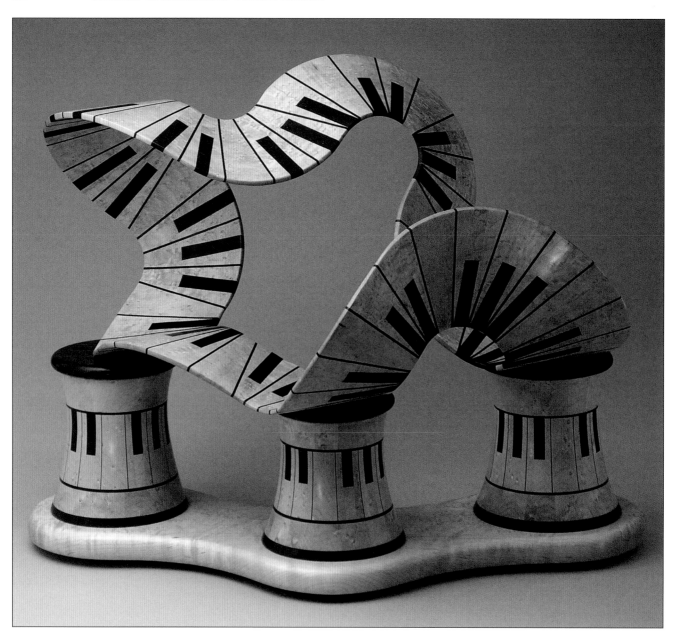

1-02   *MOBIUS SONATA,* 20 inches wide.

I have written this text for the turner who has at least some woodworking experience. You do not need to be an engineer or a mathematician, nor do you have to be a master woodworker, but familiarity with woodworking machinery and at least basic lathe-turning skills are certainly necessary. If you possess these minimal skills and are ready to take your woodturning in a new direction, then this book is for you. It is my sincere hope that I have conveyed the right mix of advice and inspiration and that I have done justice to this fascinating subject.

May all your glue joints remain perfect and may your need for challenge be completely satisfied.

Sincerely,

Malcolm J. Tibbetts

2. Types of Construction

2-01   Segments and staves are the two most common components.

The three most common methods of segmented construction are:

- the stacking of segmented rings,

- assembling staves,

- the simple lamination of wood layers.

Precise joinery and accurate glue assembly techniques are necessary for any style to be successful. You might be wondering, "What's the difference between segments and staves?" Segments are miter-cut from a board with the wood grain oriented horizontally and then the individual pieces are glued together, end grain to end grain, to form a circle or ring of wood. The individual segments can be different species of wood and they can be different lengths, and their angled miter cuts can even vary, however the

total of all their miter angles must add up to 360° to form a complete circle. The ring of segments on the right side of **photo 2-01** shows segments of two different lengths in the same ring.

The wood grain of staves, on the other hand, is usually oriented vertically like the staves of a wine barrel. Staves can be short or long, wide or narrow, and just as with horizontal segments, they do not have to all be equal, but their side angles must also add up to 360°. Segments are normally produced with simple miter cuts, whereas staves are often cut with compound miter cuts. Compound miters created the vessel under construction in the center of **photo 2-01**. If I had used simple miters to create the shape, a much thicker board would have been necessary.

So there you have it, segments and staves. These two elements compose the majority of segmented work. There are endless ways to assemble and embellish these elements, and many will be described on the following pages. Creating turnings from a simple laminated block of wood layers is also occasionally used as a method of construction. Most woodworkers already know how to make simple laminations, so I will not be focusing on this technique.

People often confuse segmented work with inlaid work. The public seems to be more familiar with the term "inlaid." There is a big difference. Inlaying is the process of creating a recessed cavity for the insertion of another piece of wood. There are opportunities for this technique in segmented work, although most assembly involves layering thicker pieces of wood together, thereby creating the same design on the inside as well as the outside of the turning. For example, suppose you wanted a diamond shape of light-colored wood surrounded by darker wood. To inlay, you would cut a recess into the surface of the darker wood (by hand or router) and then glue a thin but accurately shaped piece of the light-colored wood into the recess. To laminate the diamond shape into a turning requires a different approach. You start with a diamond-shaped piece of wood the same thickness as the rest of your turning components and then glue the surrounding dark wood to the diamond's four sides, using the disc sander to create tight glue lines. This assembly is then machined into a segment to be built into a ring of segments. The diamond shape will be visible on the inside of your turning as well as on the outside. Making diamond shapes is detailed in Chapter 11.

The technique known as "open segmented" has gained popularity in recent years. This style of construction creates air gaps between individual segments during assembly. I have little experience with this technique and will not be offering advice on this subject. William Smith has written a very detailed book, *Segmented Turning* (Schiffer Publishing), which I recommend to those who wish to investigate this style of segmentation.

2-02   *EMT VASE* (18 inches tall).

3-01 These are a few of my small hand tools.

3.

Tools

Segmented woodturning requires an extensive woodshop of tools. The major tools that you need are a table saw and a lathe. The size of your saw and lathe will dictate the size limitations on your work. A 10-inch table saw and a mid-sized lathe are adequate for most designs. As for myself, I have created many very large turnings that would have been very difficult or impossible on a smaller lathe. In addition, I mill much of my own lumber from very large planks and a 10-inch table saw would be undersized.

Of course, the more complex your turnings become, the more extensive your tool requirements will become and to produce quality work, you also need:

- a 12-inch disc sander (or larger),

- a surface planer, and

- a jointer.

Moreover, if you can afford it and have the space, then these come in very handy:

- a 10-inch miter chop saw,

- a 14-inch band saw (with riser block),

- a drill press, and

- a drum-style thickness sander.

In addition to the jointer/planer, a drum sander is invaluable for dimensioning thin material. It is a luxury for any home shop, to be sure, but I now wonder how I ever got along without one. If a name-brand tool is not in your budget, there are ways to construct a homemade drum sander, which you might want to investigate. Before gluing up multi-layered laminations that need to be extremely consistent, I run my strips through the drum sander. This not only provides the needed thickness accuracy, but the smooth surfaces also result in cleaner glue lines.

3-02   *CRIBBAGE BOARD* (16 inches diameter).

After acquiring tools for more than 30 years for my own small shop, it is so full that I hardly have room to move around freely. Mobile bases under the band saw, drill press, jointer/planer, disc sander, and drum sander allow me to maximize the use of my 250 square feet of floor space. It is small and crowded, but I am thankful to have it.

In addition to large power tools, you will need a variety of smaller power tools. Again, it depends upon just what kind of work you are planning to attempt, but I would say that for one reason or another, I often need:

- a 3/8-inch drill motor,
- palm sander,
- a router,
- a hand-held power-plane,
- a jig saw,
- a belt sander.

Other small hand tools that are necessary:

- lots of several types of clamps,
- calipers for measuring,
- a compass for drawing circles,
- a good quality steel straight edge,
- a small, bright flashlight,
- a trustworthy moisture meter, and
- all the standard small hand tools (screwdrivers, hammers, etc.).

Photo 3-01 shows a few of my own small tools.

The assembly of segmented work requires good eyesight along with very good lighting. When you need sunglasses in your shop, then you probably have just about enough light. I use a combination of incandescent bulbs and halogen fixtures. Make your work area as bright as reasonably possible; a magnifying light can be very useful during small-component assembly.

4-01   Personal protection equipment is essential. Turners should seriously consider the use of an air helmet system — your lungs will thank you.

4.

Safety

There are literally hundreds of ways for shop accidents to occur. Woodworking clubs are full of members who have had close calls or serious accidents. So, how do you avoid becoming an accident statistic? BE CAREFUL! This probably sounds simplistic, but I truly believe that the most effective safety tool that you possess is the six inches between your ears. Think, think, think, and when you find yourself not thinking, then take a break or maybe end your session. I am not a safety expert, but I have been around the construction trades most of my life and most of the injuries that I have investigated were due either to poor judgment, lack of concentration, fatigue, failure to use personal protection equipment, or more commonly, a combination of all four. Rarely is it the

equipment's fault. Some of my own personal protection equipment is shown in **photo 4-01**. This equipment is designed to protect your eyes, face, ears, lungs, and in the case of the anti-shock gloves, your hands (I suffer from non-woodturning related carpal tunnel syndrome). Use this type equipment if you have it and acquire it if you lack it. An air helmet system is a big investment, but is invaluable at times. It is far superior to a cloth-type respirator.

Some of the work required to produce segmented pieces can be rather monotonous. How do you keep your concentration while cutting hundreds (or thousands) of segments? I break up the work. I cut segments for a while, I sand for a while, I glue up a few components, then I go back and cut more segments. I never spend hours trying to focus on just the cutting of hundreds of segments. I keep mixing up the workload. This helps keep my mind focused on the job at hand, it keeps my mind in the game. As a segmented turner, you have the dangers of many power tools in addition to the dangers of the lathe. Take the time to devise whatever kind of jig is necessary in order to avoid putting your hands near moving saw blades, drill bits, sanding discs, etc. A very general piece of advice: if you have to cut or drill or sand a very small piece of material, then attach it to a larger piece that can be safely held. It is really quite simple if you stop and think about it: if your hands are never very close to a moving saw blade, then it is difficult to cut your finger. In addition, instead of looking for your safety glasses when you think you need them, just make it a habit to always put on eye protection upon entering your shop.

For many years, I managed outdoor operations at a major ski resort and as such, I was responsible for the safety of hundreds of employees. A few additional things that I learned about safety are:

- if you allow a dangerous condition to exist, you will eventually have an accident;

- a messy work place is a dangerous work place;

- the one time you neglect to put on your safety glasses is the time something flies into your eye;

- when you rush a job and take shortcuts, accidents are more likely to occur, and

- a dull tool is a dangerous tool

Of course, in addition to all the dangers of operating table saws, miter saws, and other woodworking machinery, as a woodturner you face the dangers of the lathe. The American Association of Woodturners (the AAW) has published a list of safety tips that do a very good job of covering lathe safety. The AAW, with over 10,000 members worldwide, is a great international organization dedicated to the advancement of woodturning, check them out at www.woodturner.org. With their permission and encouragement, I have included their lathe safety guidelines.

AAW Lathe Safety Guidelines

1. Safe, effective use of the wood lathe requires study and knowledge of procedures for using this tool. Read and thoroughly understand the label warning on the lathe and in the owner/operator's manual.

2. Always wear safety goggles or safety glasses that include side protection and a full-face shield when needed. Wood dust can be harmful to your respiratory system. Use a dust mask or helmet and proper ventilation (dust collection system) in dusty conditions. Wear hearing protection during extended period of operation.

3. Tie back long hair. Do not wear gloves, loose clothing, jewelry, or any dangling objects that may catch in rotating parts or accessories.

4. Check the owner/operator's manual for proper speed recommendation. Use slower speeds for larger diameter or rough pieces, and increased speed for smaller diameters and pieces that are balanced. If the lathe is shaking or vibrating, lower the speed. If the work piece vibrates, always stop the machine to check the reason.

5. Make certain that the belt guard or cover is in place. Check that all clamping devices, such as on the tailstock and tool rest, are tight.

6. Rotate your work piece by hand to make sure it clears the tool rest and bed before turning the lathe ON. Be sure that the work piece turns freely and is firmly mounted. It is always safest to turn the lathe OFF before adjusting the tool rest.

7. Exercise caution when using stock with cracks, splits, checks, bark, knots, irregular shapes, or protuberances.

8. Hold turning tools securely on the tool rest, and hold the tool in a controlled but comfortable manner. Always use a slower speed when starting until the work piece is balanced.

This helps avoid the possibility of an unbalanced piece jumping out of the lathe and striking the operator.

9. When running a lathe in reverse, it is possible for a chuck or faceplate to unscrew unless it is securely tightened on the lathe spindle.

10. Know your capabilities and limits. An experienced woodturner may be capable of techniques and procedures not recommended for beginning turners.

11. When using a faceplate, be certain the work piece is solidly mounted. When turning between centers, be certain the work piece is secure.

12. Always remove the tool rest before sanding or polishing operations.

13. Do not overreach, keep proper footing and balance at all times.

14. Keep the lathe in good repair. Check for damaged parts, alignment, binding of moving parts and other conditions that may affect its operation.

15. Keep tools sharp and clean for better and safer performance. Do not force a dull tool. Do not use a tool for a purpose not intended. Keep tools out of the reach of children.

16. Consider your work environment. Do not use the lathe in damp or wet locations. Do not use in presence of flammable liquids or gases. Keep work area well lit.

17. Stay alert. Watch what you are doing and use common sense. Do not operate tool when you are tired or under the influence of drugs or alcohol.

18. Guard against electric shock. Inspect electric cords for damage. Avoid the use of extension cords.

19. Remove chuck keys and adjusting wrenches. Form a habit of checking for these before switching on the lathe.

20. Never leave the lathe running unattended. Turn power off. Do not leave the lathe until it comes to a complete stop.

Respiratory Protection

One of the biggest hazards in any shop, mentioned in the AAW guidelines, is the nasty waste substance produced — the dust! It gets down your shirt and into your shoes and before you know it, there is a trail of it throughout your home. However that is not the worst: it also coats the inside of your lungs. Once you destroy lung tissue, the body can never regenerate it, the damage is permanent. Obviously, anything that makes you cough and choke cannot be good for you. While some wood species seem to be more harmful and irritating than others, no dust is good dust. So how do we protect ourselves? By all means necessary! In my own shop I operate a 3HP dust collection system, a ceiling-mounted dust filtration device, and a 20-inch fan mounted directly though the exterior wall right next to my lathe. When this fails to keep the air clean, I use an air helmet system or cloth-type respirator. My favorite time of the year is the summer when I can operate my large wall fan continuously, with the windows and door open, without worrying about heat loss.

Even with all these precautions I know that I have inhaled unhealthy levels of wood dust. It is so easy to be lazy and not take the time to put on the protection, especially if you know that it is only going to be dusty for a few seconds. Unfortunately, those few seconds add up and may result in health problems in the future. In the heat of battle, in the excitement of creating a new turning, and in the rush to complete the project, it is so easy to allow safety to take a back seat. No turning is worth a finger or permanent damage to your lungs.

Take your time and work safely!

5-0   *CARETTO VASE* (12 inches diameter) — caretto, purpleheart, gabon ebony.

5-01   Because of its stability, mesquite is a favorite wood for segmented work.

5.

Understanding Wood

It is very important to understand certain basic properties regarding your raw material — wood. A very good book on the subject is R. Bruce Hoadley's *Understanding Wood*. I highly recommend it to those wishing an in-depth education on the subject. Wood is a wonderful substance, but it is very different from materials such as plastic and metal. Having grown as part of a tree, it has unique characteristics and no two species are the same. For that matter, no two boards from the same tree are the same. If you have been a woodworker for any length of time, you have probably discovered some of the difficulties associated with wood. The most troublesome characteristic is **it moves**, its actual dimensions change. It expands with high humidity and it shrinks as it dries and it does not do this consistently. Each species acts and reacts a little differently. "So what?" you might ask. Well, I can tell you first hand that if you ignore this characteristic, then you will likely experience failures in some of your glue joints. The two biggest reasons for glue joint failure are:

- high wood moisture content, and

- incompatible wood grain orientation.

Moisture Content

Hoadley defines "moisture content" as "the weight of water in the cell walls and cavities of wood expressed as a percentage of oven-dry weight." In other words, if a not-so-dry piece of wood weighs 1.1 pounds, and this same piece of wood weighs only 1 pound after it has been baked in an oven until it is completely dry, then its moisture content would be 10%. If the wood that you use is not at least as dry as its environment, then it will continue to lose volume as it continues drying. Two pieces of wood on either side of a glue joint with different moisture contents will probably move differently. Glue is unable to restrict this movement and a gap or unevenness may appear between the two pieces of wood. It is common to experience some movement even when your wood is very dry. Different species can react differently to changes in their surrounding environment and even with the best of sealing finishes on your turnings, high or low humidity will eventually affect the wood. By using dry wood, you will dramatically improve your chances of producing stable turnings that will stay together. "How dry?" you ask. I would recommend never using anything above 10% moisture content and I would only use wood at 10% if all the wood were consistently the same. In general, wood in the 8% (or drier) range is much safer. Anything higher and you will be taking a risk —it is just not worth it! Do not trust your wood, just because the supplier tells you that it is "kiln dried." The wood may have been 7% moisture content when it came out of the kiln, but if it has been improperly stored in a moist environment, then it may no longer be at that percentage. **Photo 5-01** displays a recent purchase of mesquite that was imported from Argentina. This is terrific material for segmented work, because it is known for its stability, that is, its lack of movement after drying. It was described as being "kiln dried" and it probably was, but unfortunately, it came by ship and was stored for several months in a warehouse in Seattle before being purchased. I was very happy with my purchase and not terribly surprised when I measured the moisture content. It ranged dramatically from about 9% up to 14% from board to board. By the way, the main wood in the vessel on the front cover is Argentinean mesquite from that pallet.

How you store your own wood inventory is important, especially if you live in a humid climate. Your storage area obviously has to be dry. I live in the Sierra Nevada Mountains of California (Lake Tahoe) and for about half the year, we enjoy a very dry climate. Then winter comes. It can be dry one day and snowing the next. Until I built a heated drying shed with a dehumidifier, my wood inventory was always in a state of change with the seasons. I call this storage device a drying shed, not a kiln. It is just a warm, dry, low humidity, insulated, large, storage closet. During the summer months, unless I am in a hurry to use particular boards, I do not operate the heater. The outside of the shed is painted black and solar heating keeps the inside quite warm, but during the winter months, a small electric heater keeps the shed a toasty 90° and the dehumidifier runs on a regular basis. Wood that is drier than its environment will quickly acquire moisture if improperly stored, which is why you must test your wood.

Testing for Moisture Content

How do you measure the wood's moisture content? One method involves repeatedly oven-drying a sample and then weighing it until it no longer loses weight. I do not have much experience with this technique and frankly, it seems like quite a lengthy process. On the other hand, there are several manufacturers of very easy to use electronic moisture meters. These devices are able to determine the amount of water content in the wood by measuring electrical resistance between two sharp probes that you insert into the wood. Wet wood is a much better conductor of electricity than dry wood, and these meters detect this difference. Be aware, wood does not dry uniformly. The outside can be considerably drier than the inside and exposed end grain will always

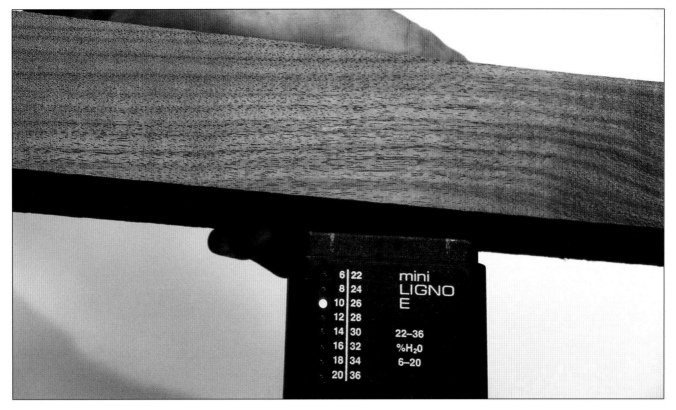

5-02   Wood must be tested for moisture content.

measure drier than the rest of the board. Actually, testing the end of a board is a waste of time. If you are ready to start your project, and you know the required width of a strip of wood, then rip-cut a strip from some of your boards and test the interior of the wood. Place the probes in line with the grain as shown in **photo 5-02** and check several locations.

What do you do if your wood is not dry enough? Imagine — you are all ready to start a new project, you have done all the design work and at the last minute, you discover that some of your wood measures 14%. Do not be tempted to proceed, you will most likely regret it later. Your only choice at that point is to continue drying the wood. Do not learn this lesson the hard way! The important messages are:

• test your wood, and

• take the necessary steps to ensure that your wood stays dry.

Importance of Wood Grain Orientation

The second and probably most common reason for glue joint failure is incompatible wood grain orientation. What do I mean? The important thing to remember is almost all wood movement is perpendicular to the direction of the wood grain. A board moves sideways, not lengthways, therefore segments move mostly up and down and in and out; they move very little from end to end.

This predictable movement is certainly a disadvantage and a nuisance, but you can design your turnings to allow all the wood to move together by orienting as much as possible all your individual pieces of wood so that all the grain is positioned the same direction. In a simple vessel composed of stacked segmented rings, this is easily accomplished. By gluing all the segments end to end, all the wood grain will be horizontal. As you stack the rings together, all the wood grain continues to remain horizontal. If the wood moves, it all moves together, without exerting opposing pressure on the glue lines. All is well and the vessel should live happily for a very long time.

Complex turnings, containing elements that are not all horizontal, present a more difficult challenge: you must minimize opposing forces during the design phase of your project. That does not mean that you cannot position two pieces of wood perpendicular to each other. In small dimensions, this can be done with confidence. The total movement within very small pieces of wood is usually not a problem. If we go back to that simple vessel with all its segments positioned horizontally and we now decide to place a thin piece of contrasting wood vertically between each segment, then this is OK if the horizontal segments are not too tall (thick). I would recommend not exceeding 3/4 inch, and that might be pushing it. I have constructed many such turnings with short vertical pieces glued between horizontal segment ends and those turnings have remained sound for many years.

However, sometimes designs require a taller vertical element next to a horizontal element. This is potential trouble! It may require extra work in the milling of your wood, but instead of gluing a thin strip of wood with its grain oriented vertically, use a short, wide piece of wood, thereby keeping all the grain in the same orientation. **Photo 5-03** shows an example of this; in this turning, large segments with portholes make up the outer apron of the table. The 1/4-inch wide strips of walnut positioned between the large segments of myrtlewood are orientated with their grain horizontal just as the large segments. Many people do not notice this type of attention and care, but your glue lines will thank you.

People with backgrounds in woodworking are sometimes surprised at the extensive use of end-grain-to-end-grain glue joints in segmented woodturning. After all, everyone knows that end-grain glue joints are not nearly as strong as side-grain glue joints. While that is certainly true, woodturnings are subjected to few external forces, it is the internal forces caused

by possible wood movement that need most of the attention. Besides, the weaker end-grain joints are usually reinforced by the overlapping side-to-side grain joints that are present between rings. By overlapping the alignment of vertical glue lines (like laying bricks), you are essentially creating a series of mortise-and-tenon type joints, which are very strong and effective.

Choosing Wood

Choosing wood for a turning can be fun. Because most of the time, relatively small quantities are required, we have the opportunity to work with exotics that otherwise might be too expensive. There are so many types of wood from which to choose. William A. Lincoln's book, *World Woods in Color* (Linden Publishing), displays more than 250 color photos of different woods. It is a great reference tool for woodworkers. My own personal experiences with the woods of the world consist of a much shorter list. I have listed below those woods with which I have had enough experience to form an opinion. These are woods that I have cut, sanded, glued and finished during the past 30 years. As you will see, I have categorized these woods into three designations — limited use, OK, and personal favorites. These are simply my personal preferences and opinions.

Limited-use woods include alder, ash, aspen, birch, lacewood, madrone, mahogany, maple (soft), oak (red & white), padauk, poplar, redwood, teak, and zebrawood. These woods just do not make the grade, they are either too soft, too oily, too open-grained, or too dull in appearance, although from time to time, in the right circumstances, I do use some of them.

OK woods include beech (spalted), birch (spalted), cherry, ironwood, limba (light and dark), osage-orange, walnut, and wenge. These woods are OK, but for one reason or another, they do not inspire the same enthusiasm as the ones listed next. I do use some of these quite a bit, but usually not as a stand-alone featured wood. Walnut and wenge provide a nice lower-

5-03   As much as possible, wood grain direction should be consistent.

cost alternative when a large volume of dark wood is required.

Personal favorites include apple, blackwood, bloodwood, bocote, bubinga, carob, ebony (Gabon), ebony (Macassar), holly, jarrah, maple (bird's-eye), maple (hard), maple (curly), maple (spalted), mesquite, mountain mahogany, myrtlewood, persimmon, pink ivory, purpleheart, rosewoods (pau ferro, East Indian, Honduras, Brazilian, cocobolo, flamewood, tulipwood), yellowheart, and ziricote. These are favorites for several reasons: they have great color and/or figure character, and except for the rosewoods they all glue well and most of them are tight-grained, which means they polish nicely.

When designing a turning, you are faced with many choices of wood. What goes with what? What combinations do not work well together? Over the years I have probably combined most of the woods listed above. The easiest and less

troublesome combinations involve woods that are similar in density — hard maple next to most any of the exotics as an example. I have to admit, I am partial to tight-grained, dense, hardwoods. They cut and sand uniformly and usually take a nice finish. Soft woods and open-grained woods, in general, just do not project the same type of look. You can certainly combine soft woods with hard woods, such as holly and ebony. However, it requires a little more diligence to achieve a smooth surface, it requires high-speed shear scraping, and you need to minimize coarse-grit sanding. Oily woods present their own special problems. They do not glue as dependably and they often shorten the lifespan of your sandpaper by quickly clogging the grit. The best advice that I can give you regarding oily woods is to glue them quickly. Do not allow the segments to sit around overnight and possibly release any extractives onto the gluing surfaces. I also caution against creating rings that consist of only oily woods such as cocobolo and teak. Gluing a wood like cocobolo to itself is much more risky than gluing cocobolo to a non-oily wood. I have heard people suggest that cleaning oily wood glue surfaces with substances such as acetone or lacquer thinner just before gluing will ensure success, but I have never found it necessary as long as the gluing is done soon after the cutting and sanding.

Some other combinations that can cause you problems are combining a wood like padauk with a wood such as holly — a bad idea. The colorful padauk dust is very effective as a staining agent and often makes a mess of adjacent light-colored wood, especially a white, soft wood like holly. You might be able to overcome this problem on the outside of your turning, but to maintain white holly on the inside is just about impossible. If you desire a red/white color contrast, a combination such as bloodwood and maple is a better choice.

Combining contrasting wood colors is a big part of segmented turning, but the sad truth is, all woods darken with age. Exposure to sunlight accelerates this darkening process. Woods that are dark to begin with will become darker and eventually will start to look alike. Therefore, it is important to choose wood combinations that will retain their contrast over time. Obviously, white and black combinations will provide the most dramatic contrast and last almost forever. Other combinations will be less dramatic and not as long-lasting. As an example, you might decide to combine a red wood such as bloodwood with purpleheart. When freshly machined they will look very nice together; however, within a few years (or less), from across a room, they will appear to be the same color and the effect that you desired will have been lost. The lesson here is, select woods that will provide long-lasting contrast if that is the effect you desire. Study your choices and try to visualize your turnings as they will appear after years of inevitable darkening.

As woodworkers, it is easy to get excited about spectacular grain in a board; however, as segmented woodturners we have the ability to create our own spectacular grain and figure effects. We do not have to purchase the biggest, most expensive boards at the store in order to create beauty. We can utilize small boards, cut-offs, and scraps at considerably less expense. I have constructed many turnings from numerous similarly colored woods in order to achieve an overall effect. In those cases, I was not as concerned with contrast as I was with the look. An example of this is shown in the photo of *TERE'S APPLE* (**photo 5-04**).

In this turning, I attempted to duplicate the shades of an actual apple by randomly using bloodwood, pink ivory, and tulipwood. This apple (a gift to my schoolteacher wife) is also a box with an outside profile that has been flattened in places to imitate an actual apple. Approach your wood selection decisions like a painter choosing colors from his palette, while keeping in mind the individual characteristics of each wood species.

In case you have not figured it out yet, I love wood. All woods are good for something. Even the sawdust we produce has value to someone. I sometimes feel like a kid at Christmas when I surface-plane rough stock and discover the hidden beauty that lies in wait. I observe gallery visitors approaching my turnings with a sense of awe and with an almost uncontrollable desire to touch the surfaces. Beautiful wood has that effect on people. I love the opportunities to share my passion with this amazing material. Perhaps this is why I became a segmented woodturner instead of an ironworker.

Preparing Your Wood

Before starting the process of cutting segments, you should accurately dimension all of your wood, or at the least, all the wood that will be needed for a particular phase of your project. This is important for several reasons: it allows you to confirm the quality and the quantity of your useable material and it saves you from having to interrupt the construction process in order to prepare more material. By preparing all your wood at the same time, you will create

5-04   *TERE'S APPLE* (4 inches tall) — think of wood colors as paint.

consistent dimensions, which will make your assembly easier and more accurate. You might be thinking that you are only going to be using small pieces so why bother truing-up the whole board. Believe it, the straightness and flatness of your boards affects the accuracy of your miter cuts. It is important to take the time using whatever technique works for you to flatten and then accurately dimension your lumber ahead of time. Using a jointer followed by a planer and sometimes even using a drum sander is my usual routine. Otherwise, during the cutting and gluing phases of your project, you will have to deal with problems such as a board that does not sit right on your saw. Think about the unpleasantness of trying to make accurate miter cuts across a board that wobbles on your saw, or think about gluing segments into a ring that do not sit flush with one another because their heights differ. At a minimum, it is a hassle, but it can also easily lead to inaccuracy. It is very difficult to build precise segmented rings from crooked boards of varying thickness.

6-01   Different glues are needed for different situations.

6.

Glue

Without the availability of effective, long-lasting, dependable glues, segmented turning could not exist. There are many different types and brands. I am often asked, "So, what is the best one?" If I could have only one type of glue in my shop, then the answer would be pretty simple — original Titebond (and the company did not pay me to say that). It is versatile and has always performed well for me, as well as many other turners that I know. However, I also use many other types of glue for a variety of tasks. Here is a list of what I use, how I use it, and a few other thoughts:

Titebond Original
I use Titebond Original (PVA, or polyvinyl acetate) glue on most all of my ring assemblies and ring stacking glue jobs. I also use it to attach turnings to faceplate-mounted waste blocks and to glue together design elements. I can flatten and stack

freshly glued ring assemblies in as little as a half hour after gluing, but I am usually not in that much of a hurry. While a glue joint may be strong enough to turn, un-cured glue squeeze-out on the sidewalls of your turnings can be messy to deal with as it gets all over your gouge and then, when sharpening your gouge, it glazes over your grinding wheel. This is difficult to avoid without waiting for hours or overnight. This glue's quick curing time is a big advantage most of the time, except for those big, time-consuming glue jobs.

Titebond Extend

Titebond extend gives me about 30% to 40% more working time depending upon temperature. I use it just as I use the original when I need more working time. I have not noticed any difference in performance compared to the original.

Epoxy

Epoxy makes a nice paste when mixed with sawdust to fill voids. Epoxy works well for small inlaid work, but for most large glue jobs, in my opinion, it is a little too brittle, not allowing the wood to move at all. Even extremely dry wood will sometimes try to move a little due to moisture content changes. I have seen epoxy fail because it had no give.

Cyanoacrylate (CA or super glue)

Super glue is great for quickly attaching small components to waste blocks. I use it to fill small cracks and voids (in the wood, not between segments). I do not use it for permanent assembly of segments or for any large attachments to waste blocks. It's an effective stiffener when soaked into soft, punky wood.

Polyurethane

Polyurethane glue sometimes is used for oily wood segment assembly. It provides longer working time than Titebond Extend. It is good glue, but messy and difficult to clean off your hands. Rubber gloves are an absolute necessity, but I still manage to get some on me and it takes days for the cured glue to wear off. Good clamping pressure is essential and 24 hours of cure time are recommended. One oddity about

this type of glue is that it is moisture activated, meaning, that it needs a little moisture to cure. Super-dry wood should be lightly moistened with a misting spray bottle before commencing the glue job.

Hot Melt (sticks)

I use hot melt often for temporary attachment of rings to waste blocks. It is easily removed with a utility knife and/or chisel. It will not hold items that protrude very far from the waste block (vibration), but I have used it to temporarily attach short rings more than 40 inches in diameter.

Spray Adhesive

I only use spray glue for the temporary attachment of sandpaper to sanding blocks. A light spray on the back of the paper, without spraying the sanding block, allows you to easily remove and change the paper.

Urea Resin

Sometimes called plastic resin, I use urea glue for large lamination jobs. It provides about 30 minutes of working time. It is a little messy and inconvenient (you have to mix it), but it has never failed to do its job.

Turning a vessel that is composed of hundreds (or thousands) of pieces of wood means that you are also turning that many glue lines. Glue is much tougher on your lathe tools than green wet wood, it blunts your cutting edges quickly. Think of turning a circumference with 24 segments with your lathe speed at 1000 rpm. That accounts for 24,000 tiny attacks on your nicely sharpened edge every minute. You will find that you need to re-sharpen much more frequently when turning glued assemblies. When purchasing turning gouges, look for the hardest steel available.

Clamping

I always try to apply some pressure to freshly glued joints in order to force all the excess glue from my joints. How does one gauge the required pressure and how much should be applied? It is probably an acquired sense, but

6-02   You can never have enough clamps.

my experiences tell me that many people try to apply too much force with their clamps. I generally never apply more clamping pressure than I could if I were applying the pressure with just my hands or weight (I weigh over 200 pounds). The manufactures of Titebond suggest as much pressure as 200 pounds per square inch; I am sure that in general, I apply far less. Remember, most of the time the total surface area is quite small. Getting the fit right is far more important and effective than cranking down on your clamps. The amount of glue that you apply is important, too much glue only requires more pressure to force the excess from the joint. Ideally, when using glue such as Titebond, only a small bead of squeeze-out should occur. A thin coating of glue on both surfaces is far more effective compared to an excess amount of glue on just one surface. Because of all the necessary cutting I generate hundreds of little pieces of scrap wood. I keep a stockpile of them available with which to spread glue.

There are many styles of clamps available and I use different types depending upon the task:

- pipe clamps for heavy duty laminations;

- bar clamps for smaller laminations;

- quick clamps (a small bar clamp with a pistol-grip tightening handle);

- spring clamps of various sizes for small parts and sometimes for joining two rings;

- rubber bands for small rings and irregularly shaped small parts;

- hose clamps for larger ring assemblies (they can be joined to form any diameter), and

- strap clamps for the really big ring assemblies.

Some of the most used clamps in my shop are rubber bands. An assortment of sizes can be cheaply acquired from any office supply store and by doubling or tripling a single band, a variety of pressures is possible. Just when I think that I have finally accumulated enough clamps, a project comes along that requires even more clamps. I do not know a woodworker who has too many clamps (**photo 6-02**).

6-03   Gluing cauls enable pressure to be applied in the right direction.

As a segmented woodturner you will spend far more time cutting, sanding, and gluing than you will turning. Meeting the challenges of creative clamping is crucial to your success. Generally, the goal is to apply pressure at a perpendicular angle to the glue line. Sometimes it is necessary to first attach gluing blocks (cauls) onto your components temporarily, thus creating the ability to apply clamping pressure in the desired direction. An example of using gluing cauls is shown in **photo 6.03**. This particular glue job required two applied cauls (MDF pieces) in order to apply the needed perpendicular pressure. Other times, you may find that it is just easier hand-holding your pieces for a few minutes. Regardless of technique, at least some momentary pressure is necessary. The components being glued in **photo 6-03** formed a feature ring for the cover vessel, *BROKEN SPIRITS*.

Glue Safety

Most people never think about glue dangers, but they should. Many of the synthetic glues such as epoxy, polyurethane, resorcinol, cyanoacrylate, and urea resin produce fumes that are quite harmful to your respiratory system. Some of these glues also produce harmful dust when sanded. I know of woodturners who have had particularly bad experiences with cyanoacrylates (super glues); these glues are handy, but you have to use extreme caution. Sticking your fingers together is minor compared to the damage that is possible to your respiratory tract. Take the time to turn on a fan, open a window, or step outside — whatever it takes to protect yourself.

While the PVAs (Titebond and others) are quite safe to use, they can eventually irritate your skin with prolonged exposure. When I am gluing many ring assemblies, I try to wash my hands frequently and I usually apply a hand cream to help protect my skin. Another glue danger that few people ever think about concerns the sharp edges that are often formed by cured PVA glue squeeze-out. I have cut myself on glue edges more than once, so be aware.

7-00   *BLACK AND WHITE TEAPOT*

7

Techniques, Tricks, and Shortcuts

This is the meat and potatoes chapter of the book. I will discuss basic construction techniques: how to cut, sand, glue, and assemble components into forms. Several jig designs are also offered — few things ensure successful woodworking joinery more than good jigs.

Cutting Segments

Using a Miter Saw

Some of my past works have contained more than 6,000 pieces of wood, hence the term, segmented woodturning. Some turners cut their segments using a table saw and a few even use a band saw (with lots of sanding), but I do 95% of my cutting on a compound sliding miter saw. It is faster, less tiresome, and safer. With good equipment and technique, I believe it is more accurate. Here is my method for accomplishing safe, accurate cuts using a miter saw:

• Start by installing a disposable zero-tolerance back fence and bed on your saw; MDF (3/4 inch or 1 inch) works well. I simply place about a 2 inch wide strip on edge against the saw back fence, with another wider strip flat on the saw bed. I secure these using a pair of small bar clamps, one at each end, that hold the flat bottom board tightly against the back fence. Relocating these each time you change the blade angle gives you a fresh saw kerf. To reduce the chances of small debris from interfering, put a small chamfer on the back top edge of the bottom board.

• I use a clamping device to hold the to-be-cut strips against the back fence. The start-up shock of your saw can cause small boards to jump slightly away from the fence, causing inaccurate cuts if they are not secured. A quick and easy

method is to spring-clamp a round piece of wood to the saw bed and position a wooden wedge between this circle and your strip of wood. I like to use small circles of 1-inch thick MDF cut with a hole saw. The wedge can be quickly removed and reinstalled between cuts, as shown in **photo 7-01** (next page). Spring-clamping the wood directly to the bed also works, but it is tiring and not as fast to change. In the photo, note that I am gang-cutting two strips at the same time.

• Make sure your strips of wood are flat and have square, parallel edges. It's difficult to make accurate miter cuts from a warped board.

• Use a stop block made from hard material, something that will not dent easily. Bevel or chamfer the bottom edge of your stop block to prevent sawdust from interfering.

• Make sure your blade is sharp. Even carbide saw blades need sharpening after a few thousand cuts.

• Use a hold-down device to prevent any movement of the cut-off segment during cutting. I use simple wooden L-shaped pieces of wood, as shown in **photo 7-01**. On large segments, there is no hold-down device as effective as your fingers. I have never seen a manufacturer's guideline for "how close is too close" regarding fingers near the saw blade. When cutting small segments (under 2 inches in length), using a handheld device is prudent. You have to make the choice regarding when not to use your fingers. If the segment is small enough to make you pause and think about it, then you should be using a device. In the set-up shown in the photo, the segments are being cut on the left of the blade. If I were left-handed, I probably would reverse the set-up.

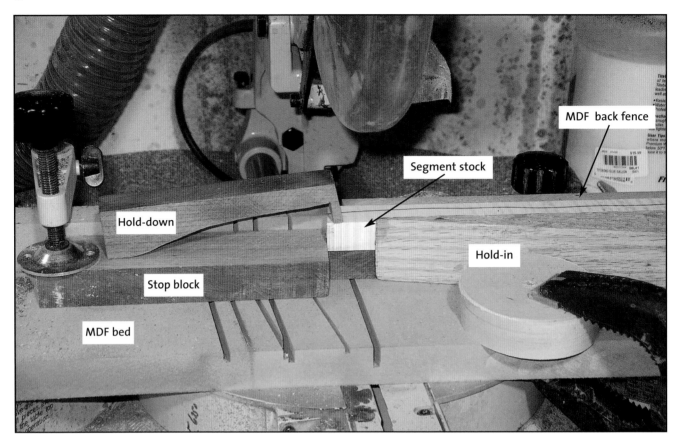

7-01   This miter-saw setup is how I cut most of my segments. Note the hold-down device.

• The miter saw blade has two chances to cut the wood: on the down push, and on the up swing. Segment-ends that move before the blade is completely retracted are liable to receive unwanted scoring. Segments can move as result of a warped wood strip, from debris under the strip, or possibly from unintentional side pressure by your hold-down device. The blade should be smoothly retracted from the wood without additional contact. The fact that the saw blade has a chance to contact the segment-end after it has been cut is the one disadvantage of using a miter saw.

• A dust extraction system connected to your saw will greatly reduce the dust interference problem and improve the air that you breathe.

• Regularly check the 90° vertical accuracy of your blade. One way to do this is to cut six rectangular segments (no miter) about 2 inches long, from a strip of scrap about 2 inches wide and 3/4-inch thick. Cut these with the strip on edge against the back fence. Lay these pieces end-to-end on a smooth surface and then turn over every other piece upside-down. Use a bar clamp to apply pressure from end to end, and observe the alignment of the segments. If your vertical blade alignment was off, the pieces of wood will not form a straight line — adjust your saw accordingly. If this is unclear, visualize a series of 5° cuts through a board. If the orientation of the cuts remained unchanged, the pieces would still fit together in a straight line, because all the cuts would be parallel to one another. By reversing every other piece, a 10° angle results at each joint. The goal is to adjust your saw's vertical angle so that any error is not detectable.

• To set your stop block to a specified segment length, make a first cut at the end of your board, then flip it over and use a caliper to make a pencil mark indicating the desired length. Line up the pencil mark with the edge of the kerf on your saw bed. Make another cut and measure the segment length, and adjust the stop block as

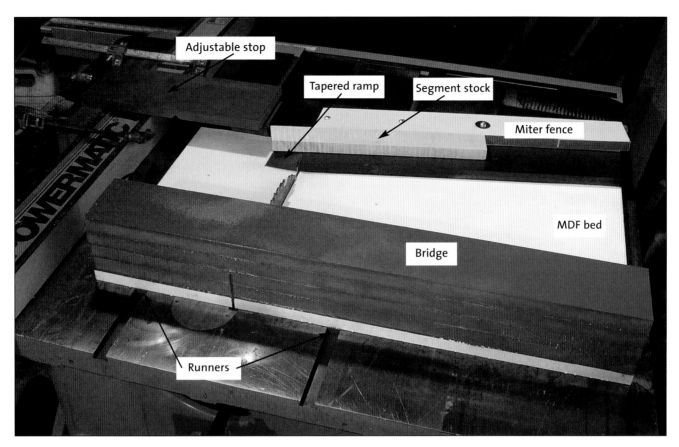

7-02   Using a cross-cut sled on the table saw is an alternative method for cutting segments

necessary. If the segments are large, I usually cut my first segment a smidgen too long and then adjust if needed, in order not to waste wood. A calculator usually displays at least five or more decimal places. Cutting segments to the nearest hundredth (plus or minus a few) is usually close enough. Calipers are much more precise than a ruler for making small measurements, however, expensive machinist calipers are not necessary.

• Once you have everything adjusted properly, it is just a matter of cutting and flipping over the strips and cutting again. Before each cut, make sure your pointed board ends are resting against the stop. It only takes one short segment to cause a ring inaccuracy.

Using a Sled on a Table Saw

Before the availability of the modern sliding compound-miter saw, the table saw was the natural choice for cutting segments and it is still a very accurate method. The goal is to make repetitive cuts that are consistent in length and angle. Using the small, 6-inch wide miter gauge that came with your table saw is a poor method; a sliding sled will improve the accuracy of crosscutting on most table saws. Some table saws are equipped with sliding tables; mine is not, so the next best thing (and maybe even better thing) is to build a sled. A sled is nothing more than a sliding surface that transports your board through the saw blade. The simplest design is just a piece of plywood with an attached miter board that is guided on one side by your table saw fence — not a very reliable design. My experience in cutting segments on a table saw is limited, but if this were my primary tool I would want a device that quickly and safely produced consistent cuts. Achieving this requires more than just a sliding piece of plywood. I built the sled in **photo 7-02** using 3/4-inch MDF, but other materials such as Baltic birch plywood could certainly be used. I have painted the various components of the sled to better convey the design and construction. The picture is taken from the front of the saw; the operator stands on the side at the top of the photo. The exact dimensions are not important so long as you understand how the device works. To build this sled:

• Start with a piece of 3/4-inch MDF or plywood big enough to span your table top from near the left side (as you stand at the saw) to several inches past the right-hand miter slot. The front-to-back dimension should be at least 20 inches. I have shown this bottom layer painted white in **photo 7-02**.

• Mill two runners that barely fit into the width of your miter slots and plane their height to slightly less than the depth of the slot. Using screws and a little glue, attach one runner parallel to one end of the sled about 3 inches from the edge. This would be the runner on the left side of the photo; the ends of the runners are painted red. With the saw blade lowered below the table, check to see if the sled will slide freely with just this first runner. Use a sanding block to loosen the fit if necessary.

• Place a couple layers of veneer into the bottom of the other miter slot, stick a piece of double-sided tape onto the top of the other runner, and trim the tape to the width of the runner. Then peel off the tape backing, and place the runner in the slot with the tape facing upward. The veneers will elevate the runner slightly above the table surface.

• Carefully position the MDF with the attached runner into its miter slot and then lower it onto the other runner. Tap the top several times to make a tight connection. Secure the second runner by drilling, countersinking, and installing three or four screws. There is no need to remove the tape.

• Place the sled back into the miter slots and check the fit. Once again, use a sanding block to adjust as necessary, creating a snug but smooth sliding fit. Grasp the outside corners of the sled and check to see if any slop exists. A snug fit is essential — an occasional spray of Teflon will keep things sliding.

• Before sliding the sled into the blade, install a bridge across its leading edge. This will stabilize the platform by keeping it rigid after you cut partially through the platform. I glued several layers of 3/4-inch MDF to create the bridge, painted blue in the photo. In addition to providing rigidity, the weight of the MDF dampens vibration, thus improving the quality of the cut.

• Slide the sled into the blade to create a kerf a little more than halfway towards the back edge.

One problem with many sled designs is the retrieval of small cut-off segments. One very dangerous option is to retrieve the segment by reaching over the blade before retracting the sled. A better solution is to use a hold-down clamp on the cut-off so you can retrieve the segment after sliding the sled back from the blade. Without holding down the segment, on most sleds you would risk the loose segment making unwanted contact with the blade. On the other hand, a hold-down adds another step to the operation and it leads to unnecessarily transporting the segment back alongside the blade. Holding down very small segments can also be difficult. Efficient cutting of hundreds of segments demands a simpler design and procedure. Ideally, segments should be easily retrieved, the length stop-block should be easily adjusted, and fingers should never be placed in jeopardy. I think these requirements have been addressed with this particular design:

Instead of screwing and gluing a miter fence board directly onto the main sled platform, install another layer of 3/4-inch MDF across the platform at the approximate angle that you want to cut segments. In this case, my goal is to cut 11.25° angles on my segment-ends in order to produce 16-segment rings. In **photos 7-02** and **7-03**, the second layer of MDF is painted green and a strip of maple sits upon it ready to be cut.

A close look at **photo 7-03** shows that the green MDF platform that holds the maple is notched back on the right side of the blade and is replaced by a small tapered piece of MDF (painted red). This tapered ramp catches the cut-off and gravity prevents further contact with the blade while the operator pulls back the sled. At no time during the cut or the retrieval do fingers need to be near the blade.

For a miter fence, use a straight piece of stable hardwood (I used oak). The angle of the oak fence, painted yellow in both photos, is critical and requires a little trial-and-error to get perfect. Using a protractor, position the miter fence board as close as you can to 11.25°. Using two large screws, attach it about 3 inches to 4 inches back from the leading edge of the second (green) layer of MDF, creating a shelf to hold strips of wood. The shelf should be as wide as any boards that you intend to cut. Secure the end nearest the blade (7.03) with a zero-tolerance screw, that is, one in a tight hole preventing side to side movement. Secure the other end with a screw that passes through a small slot in the board. This slot will allow slight angle adjustments to create a perfect 11.25°. In **photo 7-02**, the slot-installed screw is the one with the large washer. The bottom leading edge of the oak should be chamfered to prevent sawdust from interfering with the position of the to-be-cut wood strips.

During cutting, the saw blade tries to push the board away. To prevent slippage, a thin strip of 80-grit sandpaper should be adhered to the leading edge of the fence. When cutting sharper angles, install a hold-down clamp to eliminate board slippage.

An easily adjustable stop block can be created by attaching an assembly of MDF to the table saw rip fence. The exact design of the stop block depends upon your saw's rip fence. My configuration (painted blue) simply clamps onto the fence with two small bar clamps, as shown in **photo 7-02**. Instead of using MDF as the actual stop-block material, attach a more durable piece of hardwood to use as the contact surface. After building the stop-block assembly, slide it along the fence into the blade, trimming the hardwood portion parallel to the fence and blade. In **photo 7-03**, the piece of maple is positioned against the stop block (painted red). When using the sled, position the stop block on the fence in a convenient location between yourself and the blade. The stop block does not

7-03   Notice the red ramp that keeps the cut segments away from the blade.

move with the segment, it only allows consistent positioning of the board prior to each successive cut. With a stop such as this, simple adjustment of the table saw's fence easily alters the segment lengths.

Now it is simply a matter of cutting a few segments and adjusting the angle as necessary. To start this process, I cut eight segments (half a ring). I cut the segments from 3-inch wide material because inaccurate miter cuts would be more obvious than if I had used narrower material. Eight segments snugly held in a half-round shape against a straight edge will quickly display most errors. Depending upon the nature of the inaccuracy, adjust the miter board and cut 16 new segments. Secure these with a rubber band or hose clamp and once again check the seams. Continue this procedure until a ring of 16 segments can be created and held up to a light without showing any detectable faulty seams. This may take several attempts and requires patience. The slightest adjustment affects all 32 angles that make up the ring. A tenth of a degree change in the cutting angle adds up to a total change of 3.2°. Adjusting the miter board angle is really splitting hairs.

Install several additional screws to prevent future movement of the miter fence once you have achieved the perfect set of cuts.

This device is now ready to cut segments at

7-04   There are two basic ways to cut a board into segments.

11.25°, but what about the need to build a 24-segment ring or a 12-segment ring? You can either install a different fence to cut different angles, or build an entirely new sled for each different angle. This is too much hassle for me, that's why I prefer to cut segments using a miter saw.

There are several very good commercially available mitering devices. I have no meaningful experience with them, but my guess is they are not designed to quickly cut hundreds of small segments. They appear to be very good at cutting miter angles on a larger scale, and easily adjustable to different angles. For cutting hundreds (or thousands) of small pieces I think a home-made device is superior, and it sure is less expensive.

Two Methods
of Cutting Segments

A long time ago, someone figured out that if you cut a segment from the end of a board and then flipped the board upside-down, you could cut another identical segment with just one cut (and so on and so on). This common method saves time and conserves wood. However, the appearance of the resulting segments will differ from one edge of your board to the other edge and, depending upon the grain of the wood, the look can be quite different. Even if the grain was almost identical in appearance, there would

most likely be a difference in the way that light reflects from the two different surfaces. Most of the time I do not worry about this lack of consistency, nor do I often desire a perfectly matched set of segments. However, there are times when the distraction of inconsistency is unwanted. For example, a feature ring with an intricate design surrounded by a light-colored wood could lose some of its effectiveness if the light-colored wood appeared as different shades. When a consistent look is the goal, then segments must be cut another way. Instead of flipping the board over to cut another segment, it is flipped over to only cut as short a segment as possible (which is discarded) and then flipped back to the original position to cut another full-sized segment. By cutting in this manner, all the segments will have the same grain orientation and will be consistent in appearance. It also pays to label the segments to maintain the same order during gluing. This technique requires more work and it uses more wood, which is why I seldom resort to it, but sometimes the design demands the sacrifice. With some pre-planning, the short segment pieces can be used to form a different ring and thereby avoid being discarded. A simple illustration of the two methods is shown in **photo 7-04**; I used a red marking pen to represent the saw kerfs of the two methods. With this particular angle, one board produced eight segments, while the other board produced only six.

Gang-Cutting

A typical turning can require cutting hundreds of individual pieces of wood. Using a miter saw, every one of those cuts requires placing and securing the wood, turning on the saw blade, lowering the blade, raising the blade, and then removing the segment. With a little practice, this can be done quickly. However, if you can stack two or three layers of wood and cut them at the same time, then you will significantly reduce the number of operations and save yourself considerable effort. There is little difference in the cutting technique; the same care must be taken to ensure that all the pieces are against the stop block and against the fence. When cutting more than just a couple of pieces, it is helpful to wrap masking tape around the bundle of strips. There is another slight advantage to gang-cutting: the support of the adjacent layers often reduces tear-out on the underside of the wood. An example of gang-cutting two different strips, one holly and one bloodwood, is shown in **photo 7-01.**

Cutting Thin Strips

My shop is equipped with a large, 14-inch table saw, not the ideal tool for ripping extremely thin strips of wood. If you have ever attempted to push a 1/16-inch wide strip of wood between the saw blade and rip fence, then you know what I mean. The solution is to apply a general woodworking technique: if the piece is too small, attach it to something bigger. When I need to cut thin strips, I proceed as follows:

• I start by cutting a large piece MDF (at least 2 feet by 3 feet) with the fence positioned about 4 inches from the blade, but I stop cutting when the leading edge reaches the outgoing side of the saw table.

• With the MDF clamped in place on the saw table, it becomes a smooth, zero-tolerance cutting surface. This is even better than a zero-tolerance table insert, because there is no insert seam with the table surface.

• I thickness-plane a piece of wood to the same thickness as the wood from which I'll cut the thin strips. Using the MDF as the saw tabletop, I rip the wood to the same 4-inch width. This will

7-05   Cut thin strips by taping the ebony to a wider board.

be my handle or push-board.

• I adjust the fence away from the clamped piece of MDF to the desired thickness of cut. There will now be a slight gap between the fence and the MDF tabletop. The gap is no problem, since it provides an escape for any small debris that might otherwise interfere with a tight fit between push-board and the fence.

• Using masking tape, I secure my strip material to the edge of the 4-inch wide board. Usually I wrap several pieces of tape perpendicular to the board, then run a piece of tape down the entire length of the intended cut. If I am going to cut extremely thin strips (less than 1/8 inch), then I also place tape along the entire length of the underside of the two pieces of material. **Photo 7-05** shows a small board of ebony taped to a push board, being cut less than 1/8-inch wide. I can push this assembly through the saw blade smoothly and achieve a clean, accurate cut without ever endangering my fingers. It is important to maintain consistent,

7-06   Freehand disc sanding (first step) .

7-07   Freehand disc sanding (second step) .

7-08   Freehand disc sanding (wrong second step).

steady pressure against the fence to ensure a smooth and parallel cut, but because of the size of the push board, this is safely done.

I repeat the procedure as necessary. It is time-consuming and it uses a lot of masking tape, but it works extremely well and is worth the trouble: uniform, cleanly cut strips down to 1/16 inch thick, even less! If they are for a lamination, I cut them just slightly oversized and, using a transport tray, run them through the thickness sander to erase any blade markings while guaranteeing consistent thickness.

Disc Sanding

No matter how precisely you cut segments, professional results usually require disc sanding the segment-ends. When joining dark wood to dark wood, because minuscule imperfections in the glue lines can be difficult to see, sometimes it is possible to skip some sanding, but when gluing light-colored wood to light-colored wood, sanding is the only way to achieve the best-looking joints. A few turners disagree, believing that acceptable joints are possible directly from the saw blade. Many years ago Ray Allen, a well-known segmented turner, convinced me that disc sanding was worth the effort. At a presentation in Provo, Utah, he passed around two samples of glue lines between curly maple

segments. One joint had been sanded before gluing, the other had not. It was easy to see the difference. The disc sander is the only practical method that I know of for producing the best possible joints, especially when joining light-colored woods. So how is it done?

First, you need a good sander: one that runs true with minimum wobble, and whose sanding table stays locked at 90° to the disc. Not all sanders are built alike.

The sanding disc has to be sharp, not worn-out or gummed-up with wood extractives, pitch, and oils. Dull sandpaper produces poor glue surfaces and unnecessarily heats the wood, possibly causing small heat checks in the end grain.

To achieve not only good glue lines but also round rings, an accurate sanding jig is required.

If perfectly round rings are not critical, then freehand sanding can be effective, but it has to be done a certain way.

Freehand Sanding and the Rub Joint

I use both freehand and sanding-jig techniques, depending upon the size of the ring and the importance of its roundness. If I only need a small ring of consistently colored wood, such as a vessel bottom ring of ebony, I will often not use a sanding jig, however, I will still sand the segment-ends. Before sanding any segments, I dry-fit my ring together to check the fit. I can quickly determine if my angles are right-on or if they are tight to the inside or outside of the ring. I then freehand sand the segments accordingly: if the fit was tight to the inside, I apply a little more pressure to the inside of the segment-ends, and vise-versa. This is pure guesswork, the size of the segments and the type of wood both affect the pressure required. Generally, very light pressure with very little wood removal is required; I do not like heating up the wood. I am mostly interested in removing only the saw-blade markings. Applying uniform pressure from end to end takes a little practice. One exercise is to make pencil marks on a segment-end before sanding, sand just a little bit, and check to see if the pencil marks are still barely visible. Repeat this exercise until you can regularly achieve uniform removal of wood.

The goal of disc sanding is to achieve perfect glue lines, both vertically and horizontally along the miter seam. When doing any freehand sanding it is important to hold all the segments in the same relative position as they contact the spinning disc. I like to place the outside (the longer side) of every segment towards the outside of the disc; **photo 7-06** shows this orientation. After sanding the first end, to sand the second end, the segment should be flipped upside-down and end-over-end, as shown in **photo 7-07**, not rotated end-to-end as shown in **photo 7-08**. By turning the segment upside-down you effectively erase any vertical angle error, because any inaccuracy in the 90° position of your sanding table is offset. Imagine that your sanding table surface is at 89.5° to your disc. By flipping the segments during sanding, each glue joint will mate one 90.5° angle to one 89.5° angle, resulting in a perfectly tight vertical glue line. If your 90° sanding table setting is off just a tiny bit and you do not flip your segments but instead rotate them, then even if your miters form a perfect 360°, the segments will form a dish shape under clamping pressure.

When freehand sanding and gluing together pairs of segments, do not sand all the segment-

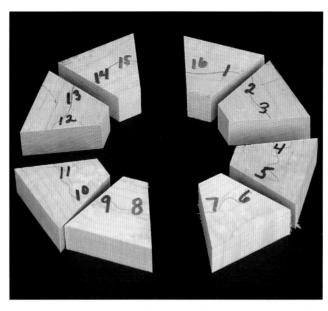

7-09   The rub-joint gluing technique starts with pairs.

ends initially; sand only the ends that are to be glued first. The sequence goes like this:

Lay out your segments in pairs, then sand only the opposing ends between each pair.

When making contact with the disc, use caution to keep the segments flush against the disc. Slide the segment a short distance (an inch or so depending upon the segment size) along the disc, being careful to maintain equal pressure against the disc from end to end. Sliding the segment reduces heat build-up and produces a better surface. A smooth (almost slippery) sanding table is essential. If your sanding table is at 90° to the disc and your miter blade was at 90° to the saw bed, then very little pressure should be required to erase all the saw-blade markings. Good cuts leave hardly any imperfections on the segment-ends.

Referring to **photo 7-09,** first only sand the surfaces of ends 1 and 2, 5 and 6, 9 and 10, and 13 and 14 (the red numbers). If you were to sand all the ends at the same time, then you would risk accidentally smearing some glue onto a sanded surface before its assembly time.

Glue each of these pairs together using the rub-joint technique.

"What's a rub joint?" you ask. This technique

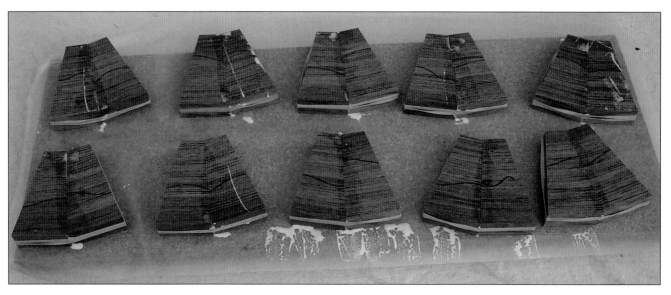

7-10   Rubber bands are optional, but recommended for large pairs.

forms good, tight joints with only momentary hand pressure. You simply apply a little PVA glue to one of the segment-ends and rub the two ends together, checking to make sure glue coats both surfaces. Then you place the pair of segments on a flat surface covered with wax paper or other non-stick surface, and keeping the segments flat, aggressively rub the two back and forth a few more times, keeping pressure on the joint, until you start to feel slight resistance, indicating the glue has begun to set. Make sure the two outside corners line up, then simply let the glue cure with no clamping pressure. Turners and joiners have used this technique successfully for many years. However, I do like to apply a little sustained pressure whenever possible, either with rubber bands around the segments as shown in **photo 7-10**, or with a clamp on large segments. Most of the time this probably is not necessary, but it can't hurt and it might result in a tighter joint.

If you attempt to apply rubber bands, you will quickly discover that you need to adjust their tension in order to apply uniform pressure across the glue surface. Experiment first with a pair of un-glued segments by pulling them apart while confined by a rubber band. The goal is to adjust the band so that it requires equal force to separate either end of the glue joint. It only takes a few tries to get the right feel for

how to apply the bands. Rub joints will set without the rubber bands, but I usually do use them on large segments.

Sometimes, after only a few seconds, you cannot readjust the alignment of two segments, so it is important to pay attention and align them accurately the first time. Soon after gluing segments together, I wipe the squeeze-out off the joint using a piece of scrap wood; this saves the sandpaper on my disc sander and accelerates the glue curing. Rub joints and freehand disc sanding go hand-in-hand.

After the glue has cured for a 15 minute minimum on the first four segment pairs, disc sand the top and bottom surfaces (the glue lines) so that the segment pairs sit flush on a smooth surface.

Now sand and glue end numbers 3 and 4 together, and 11 and 12 together (the blue numbers). During sanding, remember to orient the segments in the same position against the sanding disc. Think of the pair of glued segments as a single segment, which essentially is what they have become.

You have transformed eight segments into two half-sections. In a ring with more segments, continue until two halves exist. You may have to join just one segment at some point if your halves have an uneven number of segments.

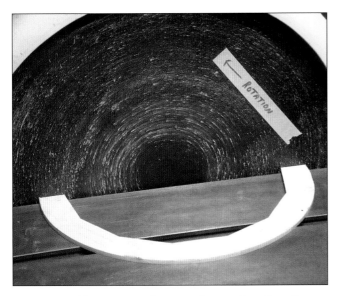

7-11   Half-rings can be trued up using the disc sander.

7-12   This ring is too large to sand both ends at one time.

If your ring is large it is a good idea to occasionally dry-fit the sections together, to check the overall fit. I usually dry-fit the final four quarter-sections to see if they are going to form two similar halves. I adjust the miters slightly by disc sanding to achieve two matching diameters before the final assembly of the half-sections. This ensures that the two half-sections will align with each other with minimal modification, thus resulting in a relatively round circle.

The final gluing of the two halves requires one last sanding of the ends, followed by an examination of the final joints with a bright light behind the joints. This final sanding job can be a little tricky depending upon the overall half-ring size, especially if the diameter of the half-sections is close to the diameter of your sanding disc. When sanding large half-rings, you will be sanding one end against the side of the disc that is rotating up with the other end on the down side, as shown in **photo 7-11**. The rotation of the disc as indicated is counter-clockwise, meaning the disc will try to pick up the right-hand end of the half-ring. This requires a firm hand on the up side to keep the half-ring in contact with the table surface so it won't be thrown.

Because the travel speed of the disc surface is faster towards the outside diameter compared to the inside diameter, more wood is sometimes removed towards the outside edge of the half-sections, causing a slight gap towards the outside of the glue joint. This is why it is important to check the fit with a bright light. If a gap does exist after very light sanding, then you have two remedies: play around with the disc sander as you sand only one end at a time (this is how I usually do it), or hand sand the ends using sandpaper adhered to a smooth, flat surface such as a piece of MDF. Hand-sanding is easiest when the sandpaper is stationary, allowing you to rub the half-sections across it. Once a good final fit is achieved, then it is simply a matter of gluing together the two halves, using hose clamps or rubber bands for pressure.

Extremely large half-rings, those larger than the diameter of the sanding disc, have to be sanded one end at a time. **Photo 7-12** shows such an example. The disc is 20 inches in diameter and the half-ring is 26 inches in diameter. An accurate surface can still be sanded, but it can require a number of trial-and-error attempts. Sand a little and check the fit repeatedly until no visible light comes through the joints.

Freehand-sanded rub joints should only be used on small rings or when perfect roundness is not critical. The method is quick and easy and produces very good joints.

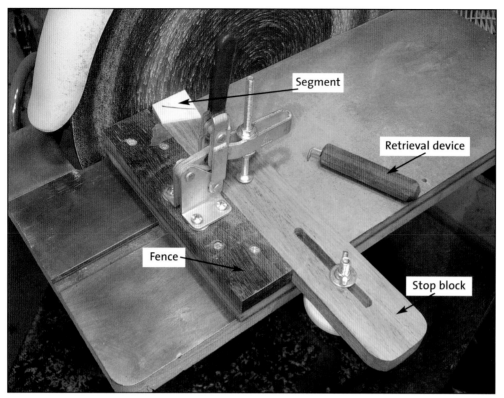

Segment

Retrieval device

Fence

Stop block

7-13   This is a typical disc sanding jig.

Building and Using a Sanding Jig

There are many designs that demand completed rings be round, not just almost round. If segments are freehand-sanded, there is a good chance that the joints could look fine but the ring could be slightly oval. Freehand sanding takes a little practice whereas the use of a jig is almost foolproof. When turning an oval ring on the lathe, several problems can occur. Valuable shape options can be lost because wall thickness will have been lost while rounding the oval shape, and design elements may not remain consistent in appearance around the ring. A sanding jig results in extremely consistent segment angles and lengths producing round rings. So, what is a sanding jig and how do you build one? **Photo 7-13** shows one of my jigs. It is important to understand that a sanding jig can only be as accurate as your disc sander. If your sanding table is not firmly anchored with its miter slot parallel to the disc, then no matter how precisely the jig is built, it will not perform as designed. Check the parallel alignment of your table slot and adjust

as necessary, and check this alignment regularly (**photo 7-14**). If your miter slot is not parallel, then your segments will be different lengths depending upon where on the disc they were sanded. Consistent lengths are as important as consistent angles.

To build a sanding jig:

• For a platform, cut a piece of MDF or Baltic birch plywood approximately the same size as your sanding table.

• Mill a miter-slot runner that snugly fits widthwise, and when placed into the slot is slightly below the table surface.

• Shim the runner with veneer scraps so that it is slightly above the table surface. Stick on a piece of double-sided tape and trim to the width of the runner.

• Carefully position the jig platform on the double-sided tape with one edge of the platform held against the sanding disc. Press the platform onto the tape to create a solid bond.

• Remove the platform to drill, countersink, and install five screws to secure the runner. The tape can stay in place.

• Check the fit of the runner in the sander slot and adjust using a sanding block as necessary. While holding the MDF firmly in place, turn on the sander and slide the platform back and forth. You should have a snug fit with the disc, but the disc's rotation should not be restricted after a few seconds of sanding action.

• Cover the runner with masking tape and drill a small hole near the center of its outside edge,

7-14   The sanding table alignment is important.

so you can hang the device. Spray several coats of vanish to protect the MDF. Strive for a smooth finish that will reduce friction with the sanding table and allow segments to slide easily. Be sure to coat both sides equally with finish, so the MDF does not warp.

• To make a fence for the sanding stop-block, mill a straight-grained piece of hardwood the same length as the width of the platform and about 2 inches to 3 inches wide; in **photo 7-13** you can see a piece of purpleheart attached to the left side of the platform. Put a small bevel along the bottom long edge that faces to the right, then use screws and glue to install the piece across the left-hand end of the platform. Strive for 90° alignment with the disc. This assumes that your disc rotation (as you face it) is counter-clockwise. If your disc rotates the other direction, then position the fence at the other end.

• The next step is the sanding stop-block, a piece of stable straight-grained hardwood (I used mesquite) with an angle at one end. Other woods are certainly adequate — I chose mesquite because it is durable and dimensionally stable. The goal is to create a perfect angle between the end of the stop block and the sanding disc. The width of the stop block depends upon the average size of your segments. If you need to sand large segments,

then the stop block should be as wide as the segments. The stop block in **photo 7-13** was created to sand segments with an 11.25° angle. The stop block angle needs to be 22.5° because it represents the overall angle of the segments (both ends). The space between the stop block and the disc represents the desired segment angle and length. Notice in **photo 7-13** that a hold-down clamp is positioned to secure the stop block to the jig platform. On this stop block, one end was cut at 22.5° and the other end was left long so an adjustable limit-stop could be installed. This adjustable limit-stop controls the amount of possible wood removal, creating consistent lengths.

• To create the limit stop, I cut a 3/8-inch wide slot about 4 inches long down the center of the stop block at the opposite end from the angle cut. The actual stop can be most anything; I used a turned circle of hardwood with a 3/8-inch hole in the center. A 3/8-inch carriage bolt was used to install the round limit stop on the underside of the sanding stop-block through the slot. The length and position of the slot should allow the angled end to be adjustable from zero to about 4 inches away from the disc, or whatever distance you predict will match your longest segments.

Here is how the jig works:

Before turning on the sander, place one segment-end against the sanding disc and the other end against the angled end of the sanding stop-block, but do not bottom out the inside corner of the segment against the stationary fence. In other words, adjust the position of the sanding stop-block so that a slight gap exists between the stationary fence and the inside corner of the segment.

Secure the sanding stop-block with the hold-down clamp and tighten the carriage bolt with the limit-stop held against the side of the platform.

Sand one end of all your identical segments by sliding the segments along the end of the stop block until they bottom out against the stationary fence. Try to alter your sanding

7-15   The stop block angle must be perfect.

avoid sanding more than necessary.

With the sanding stop-block repositioned, sand the other ends of the segments.

By now, you should have a good idea how the sanding jig works, but before using it, the sanding stop-block angle must be perfected. If you were incredibly lucky when you cut this angle, it will be exactly 22.5°. More than likely, the angle will need a little tweaking and this can require a lengthy process of trial-and-error.

To check and adjust this angle:

Cut and sand enough test segments to form a half-ring. Cut fairly wide segments, since they will show inaccuracy more clearly than small ones. In **photo 7-13** and **7-15**, the holly segment has a slash of red marker on it. This makes it easy to keep track of tops and bottoms. You can also see in **photo 7-13** the small hook tool I use to retrieve segments away from the moving disc. One of these is simple to make from a sharpened bent nail and a scrap of wood.

After sanding the segments assemble them against a straight edge and determine whether the angles are too acute or too obtuse. Hopefully, the needed correction is small and here is where things can get a little confusing. If your test half-ring is less than 180°, which means the segments are tight towards the inside, then each segment needs to be slightly more acute (or shorter on the inside). The angle between the stop block and the disc needs to be opened slightly, by placing a few layers of masking tape on the fence at the end closest to the disc. **Photo 7-13** shows how the blue tape shim affects the angle between the stop block and the disc. The addition of the tape has changed the angle of the stop block so that the next test segments will be slightly sharper in angle. If the test half-ring was more than 180°, then place the tape at the other end of the fence guide.

position by sliding the jig along the disc. If the segments are small, it's prudent to use a retrieval tool (**photo 7-13**).

With the hold-down clamp still locked, loosen the underside limit stop and place a thin shim between the limit stop and the side of the sanding sled. For a shim, I usually use a thick piece of card stock paper or a piece of thick veneer. Retighten the limit stop while holding the shim in place.

Now, loosen the stop-block clamp (the hold-down clamp seen in **photo 7-13**), remove the shim, reposition the sanding stop-block with adjustable limit-stop against the platform side, and then re-clamp with the hold-down. It is a lot simpler than it sounds. The thickness of the shim dictates the amount of adjustment towards the sanding disc, and equals the amount of wood that will be sanded off the second end. By adjusting the sanding stop-block in this manner, you will avoid having to fiddle with the adjustment. You will be able to quickly adjust for the sanding of the opposite ends, and

With the masking tape adjustment in place, adjust the sanding stop-block slightly closer to the disc, re-sand the segments, and check the ring accuracy again. Repeat the procedure until a perfect set of segments can be created. It can take a while, but time spent perfecting the jig will save much more time later.

Once the test half-ring is perfect, sand enough segments to form a complete ring. Secure the segments in a hose clamp (or rubber bands) and inspect the fit against a bright light. There should be no light visible through the seams. If necessary, tweak the angle one more time.

To finalize the angle at the end of the stop block, remove the tape shims and place one of the perfect segments against the fence. As shown in **photo 7-15**, carefully position the stop block against the segment-end and make light contact with the sanding disc to create the required perfect 22.5° angle.

This perfect angle will not remain perfect if any of the components becomes altered, most likely the alignment of the sanding table with the disc. If your rings start to show inaccuracy, check the miter slot alignment first. These instructions have resulted in a sanding stop-block for 16-segment rings. Other angles can be created using the same procedures, and one jig body can be used with an assortment of sanding stop-blocks.

While I have used sanding jigs for many years, I learned the technique of using masking tape to adjust the sanding block from Curt Theobald, a turner from Wyoming, at an AAW symposium in Pasadena, California. His trick can save you hours of adjustment fiddling and an accurate sanding jig can save you hours of ring assembly time. Frequently slide the jig to utilize the width of your disc, especially when sanding many oily segments. Reverse direction on a sanding disc is a handy feature; another set-up can be installed at the other end of the jig, thus increasing the life of the sandpaper. Do not use the jig to correct grossly inaccurate miter cuts. A saw blade removes wood much more efficiently than sandpaper, so take the time to adjust your saw as accurately as possible to minimize sanding. The gluing technique for assembling rings is discussed later in this chapter.

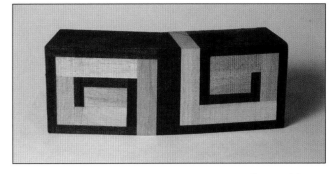

7-16   Accurate, tight glue lines are achieved by disc sanding.

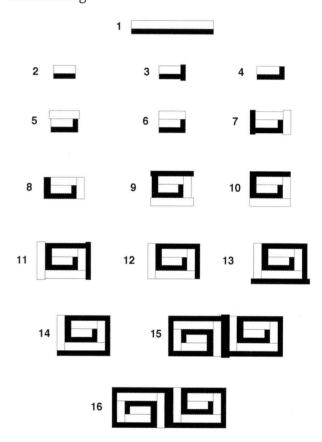

7-17   These are the individual steps to create this feature ring component.

Disc Sander Fitting Feature Ring Components

Feature ring components often require detailed planning. They can be a puzzle, requiring thought to determine the best sequence of steps. As designs become more complicated, the order in which you add pieces becomes critical. It pays to write down your plan of attack before starting. To illustrate, I will step through building the feature-ring segment in **photo 7-16**.

This is not a very complicated design compared to some — as shown in **photo 7-17,** there are 16 steps. Of course, the actual number of segments required depends upon the diameter of the ring. When making this type of feature ring, you would proceed by making all the necessary segments at the same time. For this exercise I am going to focus on the construction of the design in a single segment.

Step 1 Rip dark wood strips about 1/8 inch wide and light colored strips about 1/4 inch wide. The length of the strips depends upon how many segments are needed. Laminate one strip of each color together.

Step 2 Clean up the laminated strip and crosscut pieces 1/2 inch long. The number of pieces is twice the number of segments.

Step 3 Cut short pieces (about 1/2 inch long) of the dark wood and glue them to one end of the short laminated pieces. Cutting them a little longer provides room for alignment error. Make sure the ends extend slightly beyond the width of the first pieces so that they can be sanded to fit. Spring clamps are particularly useful for this type of clamping.

Step 4 Use a disc sander to true up the top and bottom of the assembly by sanding off the extra material, creating a nice smooth surface for the next layers.

Step 5-6 Continue this process of gluing on pieces and sanding the surfaces for the next pieces, as shown in **photo 7-17**. Whenever sanding off excess wood, be careful to keep things square and try to minimize the removal of material from the previous piece.

Step 7 Instead of adding one piece, glue on two pieces as shown.

Steps 8-14 Continue the process of sanding and adding as shown.

Step 15 Miter a center piece from dark wood, the exact angle depending upon the number of ring components. Turn one of the completed sections upside-down, and glue the three pieces together. Placing a mitered piece in the center is optional; if a parallel piece were used, then all

7-18   A bright light can help expose imperfect joints.

of the required angle would have to be inserted between the completed segments.

Step 16 Sand the top and bottom surfaces.

To assemble these segments into a ring, position another spline piece between them. The second spline can be either mitered or straight-sided, depending upon the design. Assembling rings is discussed in much more detail on the next few pages.

The key to successfully building such a ring is very precise disc sanding. It takes a little practice, so be patient. It is a good idea to build a few extra components, so you have the luxury of discarding the flawed ones. Countless designs can be built using this technique. The size of this example is fairly small, which allowed for a few glue lines of opposing grain orientation. If the same design were built in a larger size, then a few of the vertical components should be cut with horizontal grain in order to avoid conflicts in wood movement. This particular feature ring was used in the creation of *TALKING WITH WOOD*, a turning in **photo 13-16** (page 135).

7-19   Two opposite small spacers will absorb tiny mis-alignments.

7-20   Spacers help ensure two perfect half rings.

Gluing Segments Together
The Half-ring Method

With the near-perfect results of a sanding jig, segments do not have to be glued in pairs as described in the rub joint technique. A faster way, the half-ring method, can be used. It is similar to gluing all of the segments together at one time, with one big difference: two joints are not glued initially. After jig-sanding all the segment-ends, the ring should be dry-fit and checked for accuracy against a bright light, as shown in **photo 7-18**. I use a ceiling-mounted 300-watt bulb to check dry-clamped rings.

After confirming that the fit is near perfect, attach a small piece of spacer wood to the center area of two segment-ends using a little dab of glue or double-sided tape (**photo 7-19**). During the glue up these joints do not receive glue. The spacers act as a fulcrum so that any error will be taken up by the space they provide. Glue and clamp as if it was a completed ring, except the spacer joints remain dry. This is shown in **photo 7-20**. After the glue has cured, the two halves can be taken apart, touched up on the disc sander as necessary, then glued together to form a complete ring. The key to success with this technique is,the fit of all the pieces has to be near perfect, which requires using a precise sanding jig. If your angles produce two slightly oval halves, then the chances of success are much less: the pressure

of the hose clamps will try to form a circle and will likely separate a seam somewhere within the ring. If I am gluing together lots of rings in this manner, then I usually gang-cut a stack of small 1/8-inch dowels into short pieces, then attach them using just a dab of glue. The roundness of the dowels creates a very effective fulcrum.

The All-At-One-Time Method

The all-at-one-time method is just what it sounds like. It is similar to the half-ring method except there is no room for error, and errors will occasionally occur. Every joint is glued and clamped at one time. It is certainly faster than other techniques, but it is also more risky. To be successful, two conditions should apply: the dry fit of the ring should be perfect to the naked eye, and there should not be any light-colored-to-light-colored seams. The first condition is self-explanatory. The second condition (light to light) should also be easy to understand: dark woods hide seam imperfections much more effectively than light-colored woods. When gluing an entire ring at once, it only takes one segment slightly out of place to spoil the ring. If the segments fit perfectly when dry-clamped, then they will not fit perfectly when glued unless all the pieces are in the same position as they were during the test fit. Improving your chances of success requires a generous application of glue to lengthen working time, careful attention to the alignment of all the

7-21   Gluing a full ring at one time requires perfect miters and extreme care.

7-22   A rubber band gluing jig is just a board with small holes and nails.

segment corners, uniform clamping pressure all around the ring, and accomplishing the job as quickly as possible. When applying pressure around a ring of freshly glued and slippery segments, the miter angles naturally try to force all the segments away from the center, but the clamping device prevents that from happening. However, the hose clamps or rubber bands cannot pull a segment to the outside if the glue joint were to set prematurely, which would prevent the segment from sliding. A segment that is not squeezed to the outside (a misalignment of outside corners) will likely cause an unacceptable seam somewhere in the ring. **Photo 7-21** shows an all-at-once glue job. I usually limit the use of this technique to small dark rings with narrow segments.

Rubber bands are my clamping choice when clamping relatively small diameters; they apply pressure more uniformly than hose clamps and they are quick and easy to apply. Additional clamping pressure is simply a matter of applying more bands. A wide variety of rubber band sizes can be found at any office supply store; I keep several sizes on hand. When clamping very small rings (under 4-inch diameter), you also have the option of doubling or tripling a large band in order to produce the needed pressure. I have the advantage of large hands and I can stretch bands and place them around rings up to about 7 inches in diameter. Larger rings require a rubber band

gluing device. This is nothing more than a board of MDF drilled with concentric rings of small holes that accept nails. To use this jig, I place wax paper over the board and stick nails through the paper into a circle of holes slightly larger than the ring to be glued. Before applying glue to the segments, I position a rubber band around the nails. Then after applying glue to all the segment seams and placing them within the stretched band, I carefully remove the nails to entrap the ring. To apply additional bands, I keep two of the nails in place (between the band and the segments) and use them as an anchor while stretching more bands around the ring. I usually apply at least four bands, depending upon the ring diameter and the size of the bands. After applying the bands, I inspect and adjust all the segment corners, I check the evenness of the segment surfaces by using a piece of scrap wood to remove glue squeeze-out, and I flip the ring over to inspect the other side. Once I approve the fit, I hang the ring on a horizontal pipe covered with masking tape, which allows glue squeeze-out on both ring surfaces to cure. When working on a big project, I sometimes have dozens of rings hanging on pipes awaiting the next step. The rubber band clamping method works well when gluing rings up to about 10 inches in diameter. After that, the choice becomes hose clamps. **Photo 7-22** shows a sample of this gluing jig. The use of the rubber band jig is not limited to all-at-

7-23   A disc sander can be used to flatten one side of a ring.

one-time gluing jobs; I frequently use spacers and glue half-rings as previously described.

Note: Rubber bands should not be used with polyurethane glue, because it expands as it cures and requires more restraining force.

I have found that when using Titebond, I have enough time to glue up to a maximum of 36 large segments at one time (provided the temperature is cool). If the temperature is warm, then 36 is too many. When I have too many pieces within a ring to glue at one time, then I glue pairs together, thereby reducing by half, the number glue joints that I have to deal with in one operation. As a rule, I want the first joint that receives glue to remain slippery until I clamp around the whole assembly and check all the corner alignments. For the novice, let me stress: **do not attempt to close poor glue joints with extreme clamping pressure.**

Preparing Rings for Stacking

Segmented rings always need flattening before attachment to other rings. Here is how I usually do it. When I need to glue a small ring (under 14 inches diameter) onto a vessel, I usually use my 20-inch disc sander to smooth one side. My sander has a vertically adjustable sanding table that can be quickly cranked out of the way, allowing access to the entire disc. I simply handhold the ring against the disc and make a few swirling motions. 80-grit sandpaper quickly flattens and smooths the surface, thereby creating one side of a tight glue line between layers. If the ring is thin and fragile, making it difficult and/or dangerous to hold against the disc, then I make a temporary handle by hot-gluing it to an MDF backing plate, as shown in **photo 7-23**.

7-24   The 1/2-inch bowl gouge is by far my most-used cutting tool.

7-25   Checking for flatness requires a good quality straight edge..

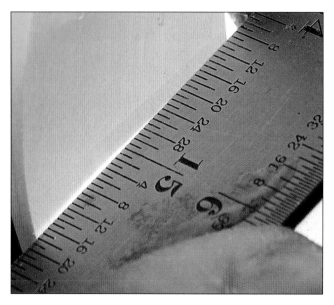

7-26   The flatness of this surface needs improvement.

7-27   This diamond-point tool is versatile, quickly resharpened, and does a great job on MDF.

There are times when the disc sanding option is not available to you. For example, as you build a vessel by stacking rings, you should flatten the uppermost ring surface on the lathe, because this will ensure that the seams remain parallel to each other. Lathe-flattening is very accurate, a little more time-consuming, and requires a little practice. Whether you are flattening a permanently glued surface, a top rim, or a temporarily mounted ring, the technique is the same. Here is how I do this:

• First, using a 1/2-inch bowl gouge, I turn away the outside and inside corners of the segments. This results in a round shape, which is simply easier to modify (**photo 7-24**).

• Next, I use my bowl gouge to smooth the glue surface. This step removes any glue squeeze-out and eliminates the ridges between segments. The exact type of cut that you use is a personal preference, just be careful to remove a minimal amount of material. A light touch of your finger

7-28   Using a flat sanding block is the final step prior to gluing the next ring.

while the ring is spinning will detect most imperfections.

• Now stop the lathe and visually (and by fingertip) inspect the surface. If the surface is smooth, I place a steel straight edge across the surface from side to side. Smoothness and flatness are not the same thing. By holding a small bright flashlight under the straight edge, I can inspect the surface for flatness. To achieve a tight glue line between layers, the two surfaces have to be perfectly flat.

• Depending upon the results of my inspection, I shave a little more wood off the highest area. **Photos 7-25** and **7-26** show the difference between acceptable and not quite close enough. The straight edge has to be extremely straight and you have to take a very close look at the contact between it and the ring surface. My goal is to achieve a perfectly consistent light transfer from the underside.

• At this stage, to make tiny final adjustments, I often switch to a small diamond-pointed scraper in an angled shear-scraping position to perfect the surface (**photo 7-27**). This small tool, with its slightly curved cutting edge, allows me to remove very tiny shavings. It may take three or more attempts to get it right. When lathe-flattening an extra wide segment ring (2 inches to 4 inches from outside to inside), the process usually requires even more attempts.

I cannot overly stress the importance of accurate ring flattening. I am talking about smidgens (the smallest difference detectable by the naked eye). In **photos 7-25** and **7-26**, the surface of the ebony ring is ready, while the holly ring needs just a little more shaved off towards the inside. If you make the slightest compromise, you risk contact between two imperfect surfaces, and then the error could become doubled and very unacceptable. The

7-29   Using a clamp against the ceiling is one way to join rings.

surface imperfections; before sanding, the surface should be as good as you could get it. When touching and removing the sanding block from the spinning ring, avoid rounding the edges of the ring surface. When I first started using the technique, I was so concerned with possibly rounding an edge that I would start and stop the lathe before applying or removing the sanding block. I no longer stop and start, but I am careful to maintain the parallel alignment of sandpaper to ring surfaces. Replace the sandpaper frequently, it is a tool and like your gouge it needs to be sharp.

lathe cutting tool and the technique that you use is not nearly as important as the result. Use what you are comfortable and familiar with. Just be sure to closely inspect the surface and avoid any compromises.

The final step in preparing the surface for gluing is to hold a sanding block (**photo 7-28**) across the ring from one side to the opposite side, with the lathe turning at a moderate speed. I use 80-grit paper, attached with spray adhesive to either 3/4-inch or 1-inch MDF. When flattening a large-diameter ring, I like to use 1-inch MDF with a piece of sandpaper attached to each end. Having several different sized blocks on hand is a good practice — you would not want to try sanding a 2-inch diameter ring with a 24-inch sanding block. If you spray a light coating of adhesive on the back of the sandpaper, it will hold, while being easily removed later for replacement. If you have done a good job with your lathe tools, then just a few seconds of sanding should eliminate any remaining imperfections on the gluing surface. Do not rely on the sanding block to correct large

Clamping Techniques

Over the years I have devised many ways to glue and clamp rings together. Extreme pressure is not necessary, but the accurate centering of the rings to each other, and the vertical alignment of the seams, are important. To glue an un-mounted ring onto a mounted ring, the easiest method is to simply place the un-mounted ring on a table surface with wax paper and a rubber router pad under it, apply glue to both sides of the joint, and place the mounted ring (or turning) on top, as shown in **photo 7-29**. Moderate clamping pressure can be applied using a push style clamp or by just stacking some weight. Before applying glue, I always dry fit and determine the rotational orientation of the two rings. A pair of dividers will help determine the center location between segment-ends. I make a pair of pencil marks once I finalize the desired position, or I apply a piece of masking tape cut at the seam. Accurate centering of the two rings can be achieved by

7-30   Using your lathe's tailstock works well for centering and clamping.

measuring the distance between the two outside diameters during the dry fit. Adjust the position until the distance is equal on all sides and make a note of this measurement. Now during the gluing you have to align the pencil marks and check the outside measurement in a couple of locations. If the difference in diameters is small, the centering can usually be done by eye-balling and/or using your finger tips to gauge the ring positions. Use plenty of glue, which will give you a little more adjusting time. Apply moderate clamping pressure and make sure the two surfaces do not slide out of position. If they do slide, adjust the clamp angle until they stay in place. The amount of pressure need not be great, between 100 and 300 pounds depending upon the total surface area, enough to force the excess glue from the seam and produce tight contact between the surfaces.

I use various techniques for gluing layers together. The previous example involved joining an un-mounted (multi-sided) ring to a vessel under construction. Another method involves using the lathe as your clamping device to join a mounted ring. After flattening the ring, using either the disc sander or the lathe, it is dry fit, aligned, marked, and glued as shown in **photo 7-30**. If I am joining a larger ring to a smaller ring, I usually turn the mating surfaces close to the same diameters, which simplifies the centering and reduces the ring width that needs flattening. The technique of using the lathe tailstock as a clamping/centering device works extremely well. It ties up the lathe for a few minutes, but usually I have something else to work on while I wait for the glue to partially cure. The ring to be added does not have to be lathe-turned round in order to use this technique. Any ring that has been center-mounted and flattened on a round circle of MDF with a center-drilled hole can be pressed onto a lathe-mounted ring by positioning the tailstock center in the center hole.

Before applying glue, always perform a dry fit, determine the rotational alignment, and make a couple of pencil marks. Apply glue to both surfaces and then bring the tailstock into place to hold one ring against the other. Apply slight pressure while twisting the two rings back and

7-31   Unmounted thin rings can be joined with spring clamps.

forth. This spreads the glue evenly, same as a rub joint. Align the two pencil marks and apply additional pressure using the tailstock tightening-handle. **Photo 7-30** shows the two pencil marks on the bubinga and holly. If you are in a hurry and the temperature is warm, you can remove the assembly from the lathe after about ten minutes. This gluing technique works well on small- to medium-sized rings.

Segmented forms can contain dozens of layers. It is not necessary to join those layers one at a time. To speed up the process, consider joining two rings to form a thicker ring. After using either the disc sander or the lathe to flatten the mating surfaces, rings can be clamped together with spring clamps as shown in **photo 7-31**.

Uses of MDF (Medium Density Fiberboard)

The design of small turnings usually calls for small, short rings; to speed up the process of consolidating dozens of small rings, I have devised a technique using MDF circles. I create MDF discs using large hole saws on a drill press, because the hole saw cuts a round disc with a centered 1/4-inch hole. By enlarging the center hole to 5/16 inch, it accommodates 5/16-inch bolts or all-thread, which when fed through the holes, automatically centers the two rings. By centering and attaching rings onto these MDF circles, I can bolt them together without being concerned about the centering, thus allowing my attention to focus on rotational alignment. Using a single carriage bolt, a couple of washers, and a wing nut, I can join flattened rings together very quickly and accurately. By gluing

7-32   MDF circles are very handy as temporary waste blocks.

7-33   A centered bolt and nut works well for clamping small rings.

hole-sawn circles onto larger circles of MDF, I can mount, disc-sand, and glue together larger pairs of rings very easily. An assortment of MDF circles is shown in **photo 7-32**. By using only small beads of hot-melt glue, rings can be removed easily from these circles and thus many repeat uses are possible. In **photo 7-33**, I am joining a single ring onto a stack of previously glued rings. On the underside of the stack, another 3-inch diameter MDF circle acts as a means to lathe-mount the assembly using a four-jaw chuck. In the photo, the underside MDF circle is clamped in a vise, which makes it possible to twist the upper MDF circle using a large pair of groove-joint pliers. After the glue job shown has cured, the assembly will be lathe-mounted, the smaller-end MDF circle will be removed, and the next glue surface will be lathe-flattened. Then another ring that has been disc-sander flattened will be joined, just as shown in **photo 7-33**. This technique is a big timesaver when faced with consolidating many rings. More examples of this technique are shown in Chapter 12.

A few tips about hole-sawing MDF circles:

• Use a relatively slow drill-press speed.

• Orient the hole saw edge slightly outside the edge of the MDF board so that it creates an escape for the sawdust. This is essential, otherwise, you will generate too much heat.

• Set the stop on your drill press quill so that you cut almost all the way through the material, but not quite.

• Flip the board over to complete the cut, which makes it easy to remove the disc from the hole saw. With a little practice, the cut disc can be retrieved without stopping the drill.

• Cutting all the way through from one side traps the circle deep inside the hole saw and requires tedious removal.

I use a lot of MDF in both 3/4-inch and 1-inch thickness, it is relatively inexpensive and extremely versatile. However, it is also full of chemical adhesives that produce very unpleasant sawdust. A good dust mask and a dust extraction system are essential. MDF glues and holds screws well, making it ideal for jig building as well as for lathe-mounted waste blocks. If you are not familiar with MDF, think of super-smooth particleboard made from wood dust instead of from wood chips. I should

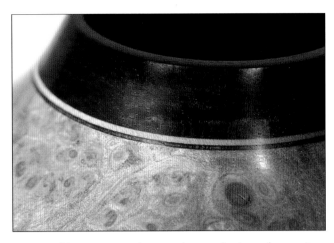

7-34   Veneers can be used as a design element.

7-35   Veneer strips stacked between MDF cauls can be quickly cut into segments.

7-36   Using veneer segments (as opposed to one piece) maintains consistent grain alignment.

caution you however: MDF should not be used as a waste block for large items unless it is penetrated by numerous mounting screws. For example, do not glue a circle of MDF to a large turning and then mount it in a four-jaw chuck, because the MDF is liable to delaminate without reinforcing screws. Number 14 pan-head screws in various lengths are usually my choice for attaching faceplates.

Working with Veneer

Veneer commonly provides a contrasting narrow band of color. **Photo 7-34** shows an example of veneer near the top rim of a vessel. Adding an occasional thin, contrasting band can dramatically improve a turning's appearance. Even though veneer is quite thin, it has grain direction and should be oriented as you would orient thicker pieces of wood. If you desire to place a horizontal layer of veneer between two thicker rings of wood, then it should be mitered together the same as the other segments to maintain uniform grain direction. It would certainly be a lot easier to glue one large piece of veneer, thereby saving time and hassle, and with a very small diameter, this is probably not a problem. With larger diameters, and therefore longer segments, it would be risky. Also, with just one piece of light-colored veneer, the two sides with exposed end grain would appear darker than the other two sides. Mostly, I use maple and holly veneer for light contrast, and ebon-x or walnut for dark contrast. I typically keep a supply of veneer strips stacked between two pieces of MDF or particleboard and tightly secured with masking tape (**photo 7-35**). When I need a ring of veneer segments, I gang-cut them on the miter saw. The saw blade will sometimes fracture a few pieces, so it is a good idea to always cut a few extra.

To assemble veneer segments into a ring, use masking tape, not glue. Position the segments on a smooth MDF surface and apply a small piece of tape to hold each joint tightly together. Masking tape does not have much stretch, but by holding down one end of the tape on one segment and pulling it onto the other, slight pressure can be applied between the veneer segment-ends. One at a time, tape the segments together until two separate halves exist. The fit of the two halves will sometimes require a little touch-up on the disc sander and then they too can be taped together to form a complete ring. In **photo 7-36**, I show an eight-piece veneer ring in the process of being taped together. The veneer segments were gang-cut on the miter saw at 22.5° to form the complete circle. The four segments at the bottom of **photo 7-36** have been taped together end-to-end to form half of the ring. After joining the other four segments, the fit of the two halves will be checked and adjusted as necessary.

Firm, consistent clamping pressure is required to glue veneer rings onto another surface. Place a thin piece of rubber (a router pad works well) on a smooth surface. Put a piece of wax paper on the rubber pad and place the veneer ring on the wax paper, taped side down. Spread glue onto both surfaces and clamp the joint with slightly more than normal pressure. I use my workbench with a push clamp from the ceiling, but many other clamping techniques are possible. It is important that before applying glue you check the evenness of all the veneer segments, because an overlapped piece of veneer will ruin the joint. The rubber pad ensures uniform distribution of clamping pressure to all of the veneer segments. If one of the veneer pieces were just slightly thicker or thinner, then without the rubber pad a poor glue line could result. The rubber pad takes up any differences. To prepare the veneer layer for the next ring in the turning, use a lathe tool to cut away the overhanging excess veneer and lightly touch up with a sanding block.

How to Make Ebon-x
Black veneer is expensive and not commonly available, that's why I create my own by dyeing walnut veneer, otherwise known as ebon-x. This is the only time I ever alter the natural colors of any of my wood. It's a simple process:

• Cut walnut veneer into pieces that will fit into a large baking dish (9 inch by 13 inch by 2 inch works). If you require larger pieces, then use a larger container.

7-37   Making two rings from one can save time.

• Make a solution of apple cider vinegar and iron filings. I shred a pad of rusted steel wool and let it soak in the vinegar for a few days, shaking it occasionally.

• Stack the veneer in the baking dish, one piece at a time, while pouring the solution onto the sheets, making sure that all surfaces receive a coating.

• Top off the pan with any remaining solution, cover with a piece of plastic wrap and soak the veneer for a couple of days.

• Remove the veneer one sheet at a time and stack the pieces neatly with a white paper towel sandwiched between each sheet. Place a flat board onto the top of the stack and weight it, or clamp it together.

• Allow the wet veneers to thoroughly dry, which can take several weeks.

Splitting Rings into Multiple Rings
This opportunity frequently presents itself, especially in small turnings. Imagine a vessel

7-38   Small plugs can be used in vessel bases.

7-39   Make tapered openings for plugs.

design that calls for many short (less than 1/2-inch tall) rings. By first constructing 1-inch tall rings and then splitting each into two rings, you will reduce ring construction time (**photo 7-37**). To split small rings on the lathe.

• Disc-sand both horizontal surfaces, then use hot-melt glue to center-mount a round piece of MDF on each surface. The MDF circles should be small enough to fit in a four-jaw chuck, or should have a center-drilled hole that fits a screw chuck.

• Mount the assembly and turn the outside profile round. Use a parting tool to separate the ring into two halves. Sometimes, when faced with the splitting of fragile rings, instead of completely parting the rings, I only cut about halfway through with the parting tool and use a band saw to complete the cut. This avoids the risk of catching a separated half-ring. Cutting round objects on a band saw is not a recommended practice; however, it can be safely done using the handles that the MDF circles provide. In **photo 7-37**, a 12-inch ring of ebony segments is being parted. In this situation I do not want to cut all the way through the ring for fear of losing the tailstock portion. Therefore, I only part halfway through and then use the band saw or handsaw to complete the separation.

The result is two mounted and centered rings. These rings are available for use as any other rings. Using them on opposite sides of a feature ring is one option. Look for these opportunities and save yourself ring assembly time and effort. In chapter 12, another method of ring splitting using a table saw is demonstrated.

Vessel Bases

Tapered Plugs

There are three basic ways to construct the bottom of a vessel: for small bases I use a solid piece of wood upon which layers of rings are attached, for slightly larger bases I like a ring of segments surrounding a tapered plug, and for large bases, a floating disc-shaped plug works best. The goal is to create an assembly that will not become over-stressed due to inevitable wood movement.

Many segmented turners build all of their vessels by starting with a solid piece of wood, and you might be thinking, "Why not?" When constructing small turnings with small bases, there is probably little reason not to start in that manner. However, I prefer the tapered plug technique. It avoids the exposure of end grain, which a solid piece of wood displays, and I just think it looks better. Remember, changes in moisture content will result in movement perpendicular to the grain direction (Chapter 5). A small plug inside a wide ring of segments is going to move less than a large and wide solid piece of wood. In addition, if you use a wide solid piece of wood alone, then the two sides displaying end-grain will often finish in a darker color compared to the other two sides.

Another consideration is the type of wood you select for the vessel bottom: you want very stable wood. Study the grain patterns and try to select wood that is quarter-sawn. Examine the ends of a few boards and if possible use something that displays growth rings parallel to the edge of the board, as opposed to growth rings parallel to the surface of the board. Generally, this type of grain orientation is more stable and the piece of wood will move less with humidity changes.

Accurately fitting a plug into a ring of segments requires a little patience. Start by using calipers to check the diameter and enlarge the inside of the ring close to the desired plug diameter with a slight taper, then turn a slightly tapered plug a little larger than the ring's inside diameter. **Photo 7-38** shows a small tapered holly plug ready to be glued into a base ring.

Now, remount the base ring on the lathe and carefully remove material, checking the fit frequently. As you get closer to a good fit, you also need to create matching taper angles so that the fit looks good on both the inside and outside of the vessel. To do this, make sure that the bottom or narrowest part of the fit is tight first and then take very small cuts until the top of the fit comes together. If you first concentrate on the outside fit, then you have no way of determining the accuracy of the fit on the other side.

Another technique, once you are very close to a good fit, involves inserting the plug into the ring while the lathe is spinning. This will immediately indicate the location of any tightness by slightly burning the plug. You should use this procedure very carefully because the plug can be grabbed and torn from

your hands. Keep a firm grip and insert the plug with extreme gentleness. Also, try not to create dark burn marks, which will harm the glue joint. If a dark burn does occur, stop working on the ring and remount the plug to remove the burn. In general, I try to avoid using this technique because burnished wood does not glue reliably.

When doing the final fitting of a plug such as this, I like to use a small diamond-pointed scraper, which I grind from 3/8-inch square turning steel. In a shear scraping position, it allows me to take very small cuts and gives me the necessary control (**photo 7-39**). **Remember: finalize the plug shape first, and then shape the hole in the ring by very gradually enlarging the bottom of the hole until the top seam comes together.**

Floating Discs

In the past, about the only glueline stability problems that I have experienced have been in the base ring area. Over time, a few large sized plugs have split or separated from their surrounding ring. Even though the plugs were relatively small (under 4 inches), the wood grain was restricted from movement and the resulting stress caused an unsightly defect. While this has not been a common occurrence, just once is one too many. I happened to mention this problem to a good friend, Bruce Friederich, who is a very accomplished turner in Auburn, California. Most of Bruce's work is with solid wood, not segmented, but he got me thinking about using a different technique. He casually suggested, "Why don't you just make the base float?" Cabinetmakers have addressed predictable wood movement problems for centuries by using frame-and-panel construction, so why not use the same principles in the base of a vessel? This has since become my preferred method of constructing large vessel bases.

This type of base plug is actually easier to build than a precisely fitted plug. The procedure is as follows:

• First, build the base ring. Lathe-mount it and

7-40   Large bases require a floating plug.

7-41   Glue only where the arrows point.

turn it round both inside and outside.

• Turn a recessed groove about 1/4 inch deep and 1/4 inch wide into the inside of the ring. **Photo 7-40** shows an ebony ring with this type of groove.

• Turn a round, 1/4-inch thick disc of wood to fit inside this groove (**photo 7-40**). Use quarter-sawn material if possible. The fit should not be tight, about a 1/16-inch gap should exist

between the disc and the side of the groove. The disc shown in **photo 7-40** will be flipped upside-down when it is inserted into the groove. Using only two small dabs of glue at each end-grain side of the plug, secure the disc into the center of the groove, making sure an equal gap exist on each side (**photo 7-41**). In the two photos I have indicated the gluing locations. Prior to gluing the disc into place, I also apply a coat of paste wax to its edge. This seals the wood and helps keep glue from sticking to the edge during the next glue job.

• Now, turn the base ring and the outside 1/2 inch of the disc flat and smooth, and turn the center portion of the disc slightly concave so that it does not interfere with the fit of the next ring. Be gentle, because the disc is only held in place by two small dabs of glue.

• To ensure that the disc remains free to move, before gluing on the next ring apply a little paste wax around its outside surface. If you look closely at the disc in **photo 7-41**, you can see the discoloration of wax around the circumference. Use a Q-tip to apply the wax and be careful to avoid smearing any wax onto the outside ring.

• Prepare the next ring. Its inside diameter

should be smaller than the diameter of the disc, thereby hiding the open seam. In this example, the next ring is shown in the background of **photo 7-41**.

• The next step is to glue the adjoining ring into place. Use a minimum amount of glue and spread it very thin near the expansion gap. The goal is to prevent glue squeeze-out from entering the gap and restricting the disc's movement. The only glue that should contact the disc should be the two dabs that hold it in place.

When using this technique, the final dimensions and shape of the vessel profile and the position of the disc must be well planned. During the final shaping of the vessel's exterior, you certainly would not want to cut though to the inside disc groove. This type of plug also requires that the shape of the vessel's bottom contain a depression, you cannot turn the base flat.

This method allows the plug to shrink and swell, and it allows the vessel walls to move independently — a simple but very effective solution to a very annoying problem. You never know what might result from communication with fellow woodturners, thanks to Bruce Friederich for the suggestion.

Improving Efficiency
Like many activities, experience usually results in easier and quicker techniques. I can look back at some of my earliest work and remember how painfully slow the forms took shape. Getting faster requires analyzing all the steps that will be required and looking for opportunities to eliminate or consolidate some of them. A few examples:

• Dimension all your boards at the same time.

• When possible, stack strips of wood and gang-cut segments.

• Glue-up thick rings that can be split into multiple rings.

• Work on more than one section at a time (the top, the middle, the base, the feature ring).

• If you are making a time-consuming, complicated element that requires lots of machinery set-up time, consider making more than one. Look for opportunities to incorporate the element into other turnings.

• Make multiples of the same turning, thereby increasing efficiency (see Chapter 12, Production Turning).

• Look beyond your current project. Think about how your current activities might affect your future turnings.

8-01   *APPLEWOOD BOWL* (10 inches dia.) — simple forms still require careful planning.

8-02   *FOR THE BOY KING* (26 inches tall) — extensive disc sanding created the feature rings.

8-03   *MYRTLE MOONS* (35 inches tall) — let your imagination go wild.

8.

The Design Process

OK, you have all your tools sharp, you have cleaned your shop, and you are ready to create your first segmented turning. What do you make? The choices are endless, that's one of the great joys of segmented work. You can create just about any shape that you desire using most any type of wood that you have available. Of course, as shapes and design components become more complex, then the design process becomes more complex. The simplest designs are brick-laid open bowl shapes, but even with simple shapes and designs, accurate assembly is important. A look at **photo 8-01** shows a lidded open bowl, relatively easy to turn but still requiring careful construction and alignment of the segment ring components.

Closed forms (vessels with small top openings) are a popular choice. This shape is actually much easier to turn as a segmented piece compared to turning the shape from a solid block of wood. The reason: you can create the shape as two separate open turnings and then join the sections together. There is no struggling with turning blind or with the difficulty of removing wood though a small opening. *FOR THE BOY KING*, an example of a closed turning that was constructed in sections, is shown in **photo 8-02**.

While the vessel is certainly the most common type of form created on the lathe, you are not limited to vessel forms. Quite the contrary, sculptural forms often stand out, and receive attention and interest from the viewing public. You have endless choices of shape and color and you have the ability to combine those shapes to create anything that you desire. An example of a sculptural form, *MYRTLE MOONS*, is shown in **photo 8-03**. Be creative and feel free to take a chance. Let your imagination go wild.

Design Tips

Regardless of what type of form you choose to create, the shape is what matters most. Interesting exotic woods and patterns will not erase the pitfalls of an unpleasing shape. I recommend that you first focus on the shape above all else. Pretend that you are making a solid, black-colored form. Ask yourself, "Can the shape be improved?". Look at the lines that you design and decide if they flow smoothly. There are many different opinions regarding good form, but I think most respected turners would agree that the profile lines of your shape should usually change direction as gradually as possible. Think of a piece of string, freely suspended between two points, compared to the same piece of string with a weight attached somewhere along its length. Gravity forms a much more pleasing shape with the unweighted string. If you vary the separation and/or elevation of the two ends of the string, the shape changes, but it generally remains pleasing. Most pleasing forms can be created by combining sections of different gravity-formed curves. To emphasize this, let me say that I am a big fan of the Spanish architect Antonio Gaudi, who designed many fanciful buildings in Barcelona in the 1890s and early 1900s. One of his design techniques was to create an upside-down model of his buildings by hanging string-mounted elements above a large mirror. By viewing the mirror image, he could see his creation right side up. An example of his genius is on display at the Sagrada Familia cathedral in Barcelona. If you appreciate whimsical, innovative, intricate architectural design, then check out the work of Antonio Gaudi at any public library or bookstore. His work might even inspire you to go boldly where no other turner has gone before.

When creating vessel shapes, try to avoid a

clunky look. Strive for a vessel base that is no larger than needed for stability. A small base will often give life to your shape. One trick, which I picked up from the late Gene Pozsesi, is to create a small air gap at the edge of your vessel's base, which will give the illusion that the vessel is floating. In other words, hide the contact point between the vessel's base and the surface upon which it sits. Another tip that I picked up a long time ago from the well-known turner David Ellsworth: look at your design upside down, it should remain just as pleasing.

Vessel wall thickness has an effect and projects a feeling. There is no formula for proper wall thickness, although in general, the smaller the turning, the thinner the wall. It is also important that the wall thickness be consistent from top to bottom. The wood is going to move; inconsistent wall thicknesses could cause uneven movement and result in unwanted stress. If you think of wood movement as a percentage of its dimension, then it is logical that the smaller the dimension, the smaller the total movement. I generally strive for about 1/8 inch wall thickness on small turnings, up to about 3/8 inch on large pieces.

Good form is perhaps the most difficult aspect of woodturning to achieve and understand. I know that I continue to learn with every piece that I make. A Supreme Court justice once said he had difficulty describing pornography, but he knew it when he saw it. Good design is also difficult to describe, but quickly and easily recognized. I suggest studying the works of the masters and not just of other woodturners. Visit art museums, look at works done in ceramic and glass. Study the forms that nature creates, because naturally occurring shapes are among the very best. Do not be fooled into thinking that a spectacular piece of wood or a particularly complex segmented design will overcome an unpleasing shape.

Non-segmented woodturners study their next piece of wood before deciding what shape to turn and they make their decisions on the characteristics of that piece of wood. Segmented turners can go though a similar process. Instead of studying a block of wood, I often study my wood inventory and then design based on what I have available. If you do not own much of an inventory, then you need to analyze what is available at your supplier. You do not want to near the completion of a turning only to discover that you do not have enough wood of a particular type. While you might be able to acquire another board, its grain and coloring might not match the rest of your turning and you will regret your lack of planning. It really pays to plan ahead.

One easily made mistake is using your boards as you need them during the construction of a turning. If your boards were not sequentially cut from the same log, then their coloring probably will differ. If you use all of one board before cutting into the next board, then you run the risk of unwanted color breaks in your turning. For a more consistent look, it is better to use a little of each board as you build your rings, then the color differences will be random and the effect will be a blending of the colors.

It is very common to incorporate several different types or colors of wood into a segmented turning. That is another reason this style of turning is so much fun. The colors catch the eye and clearly separate this style from solid wood forms. It is very easy to overdo it, and I have certainly been guilty of the over-use of multiple wood types. Using many different types of wood is not always a bad thing, one just has to be aware that it can be overdone and that too many colors can result in a busy turning. Sometimes, less is better.

As you design your turnings, you must make many other decisions. One choice is the number of segments to include in each ring of the construction. This is a key decision that can have a dramatic effect on the appearance of your turning. There are no minimums or maximums, it is up to you. The advantage of fewer segments is, you will not have to cut and glue as many individual pieces of wood. However, if you choose too few, your turning may appear clunky or heavy and it may not project the desired effect to the viewer. As the number of segments per ring becomes fewer the sharpness of the ring corner joints increases, and you will have to contend with end-grain chip-out during the turning process. Conversely, the more segments per ring, the more gentle the corners and as a result, the shaping on the lathe will go more smoothly.

As a general practice, I avoid constructing rings with fewer than 10 segments, and 12 to 24 segments per ring is more the norm. On large diameters (20 plus inches), 24 to 60 segments should be considered. Even on large turnings, segments that are longer than 5 inches usually appear too big. Try to visualize the appearance before deciding upon the number of segments. Before deciding, calculate the segment lengths for both the largest and the smallest rings.

I like to maintain the same number of segments per ring throughout the turning. It is certainly possible to vary the number of segments per ring, however, I would recommend that you do it in a way that is not immediately apparent to the viewer.

Regarding staved construction, you do not have the same segment corner issues while turning the profile, but you need to select a number of staves that creates a nice proportion to the overall size of your design. A column created from only three or four staves is possible, but you might as well turn a solid block of wood. I like to construct staved vessel forms with a minimum of eight staves. A big concern with stave construction is, "How do you add any layers above or below the staved portion of the form?" The wood grain in the staves is vertical: "Do we have to maintain the same grain orientation in the other adjacent components?" In general the answer is yes, although I have to admit that I did not always do this in some of my early turnings and many of them have survived for many years, but a few have not. The success or failure of perpendicular-grain glue lines mostly depends upon the length of the joint. Short intersections of opposing grain direction are much more likely to succeed. However, when possible, avoid these types of joints. In Chapter 10, I describe, a step-by-step

8-04   Designs can be created by brick-laying different colored woods.

construction of a staved vessel and I offer a solution to the grain orientation challenge.

Feature Rings

It is common for segmented vessels to contain a feature ring within their design — a decoration that adds interest for the viewer. The number of design elements should correspond to the number of segments that comprise the other rings in the turning. For example, if I decided to construct a turning with eight Indian blanket designs positioned around it, then I would normally build the other rings with eight, sixteen, or twenty-four segments. This would allow me to align all the rings in a balanced configuration. I do not want to create a configuration that displays dramatic differences in the alignment of the vertical glue joints between layers, which would occur if all the rings were not multiples of each other. In most designs, I think a lack of symmetry between the vertical glue lines creates an unpleasing effect, although there are exceptions such as when using randomness as a design element.

What are the choices regarding feature ring designs? Here again, there are endless choices and you have the opportunity to create something that no one else has ever done. On the next few pages I offer a few possibilities.

8-05   Large diamonds require the use of a disc sander.

8-06   A router created the opening for this small diamond shape.

8-07   *ZIGZAG BOX* (3 inches diameter) — just one of many feature ring designs.

Southwest Indian pottery and basketry have had a big influence on segmented woodturning designs. Their geometric designs lend themselves very nicely to the assembly process of segmented work, which is why so many segmented turners have focused on these types of designs. Southwest designs also seem to be quite popular with the buying public, but you are certainly not limited to them. Quite the contrary, because there is so much Indian-style work being done, I encourage you to explore other possibilities.

Brick-laid designs appear relatively simple, but accurate construction and alignment of the rings is essential and in a large design, rotational alignment is very difficult to maintain. Complete vessels can be constructed in this manner, so the intricacy of your designs is completely your decision. This type of construction is very stable because all the wood grain is consistently horizontal. Successful alignment of the segments does require round rings. Rings that are just slightly oval will cause unequal segment lengths and the result will be inconsistency. In Chapter 12, a production run of six similar brick-laid vessels is presented. In addition to brick laying with equal-sized segments, unequal segment lengths also can be used. To avoid confusion during construction, you definitely need a detailed sketch from which to work.

Diamonds created with a disc sander are another choice and they are actually quite simple to make. **Photo 8-05** shows a rather large diamond design (about 2-1/2 inches wide). If you look very closely, the order of assembly can be seen. **Photo 8-06** shows a router-created diamond design; this is done very differently, requiring precise woodworking skills. The diamond in **photo 8-06** is actually less than 1/2 inch wide. See Chapter 11 for detailed instruction regarding both of these techniques.

Zigzag patterns are time-consuming, but they impress viewers. The sample in **photo 8-07** is a small, 3 inch lidded box. The lid has been removed to show the zigzag on the inside. Zigzags can be built using multiple layers, and

8-08　Indian blanket designs are easy once you know the trick.

8-09　Porthole designs require careful planning.

they can be flat or steep depending upon the miter angles. Detailed, step-by-step instruction is also presented in Chapter 11.

There are countless variations of Indian blanket designs (**photo 8-08**). These designs are easily achieved by executing numerous woodworking steps as described in Chapter 9.

If I have a signature element, it is probably portholes or segments with windows. They provide an opportunity for incorporating endless designs into your turnings. The sample shown in **photo 8-09** is quite small and displays small, 1-inch cabochons of macassar ebony. I have also used stone cabochons in some of my porthole designs. Larger windows can be used to display marquetry designs; the technique is covered in detail in Chapter 15. The curved pieces of maple in the photo result from exposing a layer within the segments, another technique covered in Chapter 13.

Feature rings are usually the focus of a turning. They grab the viewer's attention and they provide many opportunities for expressing your creativity. These few examples barely scratch the surface of possible designs. If you need more inspiration or additional ideas, investigate the public domain designs of the past. Look at ancient Egyptian art, Indian art, and computer clip art; look at product packaging, and look at the patterns that Mother Nature creates. Design

ideas surround our lives, though perhaps most satisfying are the original designs that we as artists invent.

Creating a Blueprint

In all but the simplest of designs, you must have a plan. It can be a hand-drawn sketch or a detailed computer drawing, but YOU HAVE TO HAVE A PLAN. Before creating that plan, let us review a few basic geometric principles:

● a circle contains 360 degrees.

● the circumference of a circle is equal to its diameter times pi.

● pi is equal to 3.1416.

● the diameter of a circle is equal to its circumference divided by pi.

Also,

● circumference divided by number of segments equals segment length.

● segment length times number of segments equals circumference which, when divided by pi, equals diameter.

This is most of the math that you need to know, with the exception of compound miters, which I discuss in Chapter 10. With a small calculator

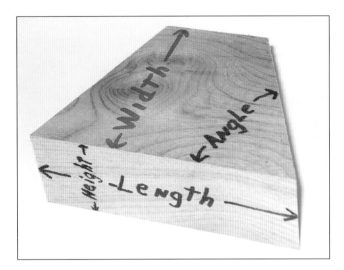

8-10   The terms can become confusing.

you can determine everything you need by doing simple multiplication and division. Just to avoid any possible confusion regarding segments, let me define and illustrate a few terms using **photo 8-10**:

• segment length: length of the long side (the outside corner to corner).

• segment width: width of board from which segments are cut.

• segment height: thickness of board from which segments are cut.

• segment angle: the angle of cut, usually 360° divided by the number of segments divided by 2 (2 angles per segment).

Here are a few additional bits of information to consider as you go about the design process. If you design a turning with rings 3/4 inch tall and you use boards that are 3/4 inch thick, then your total completed height will be less than designed. While stacking the rings, you will lose some height due to machining and sanding the horizontal surfaces between rings. I normally draw my designs to account for a 1/16-inch loss in height on each ring (less if the turning is quite small). Coincidentally, the thickness dimension of many commercially available hardwoods is 13/16 inch. In effect, the waste factor has been figured in for you. This may seem insignificant, but with a tall turning, it can add up and distort the designed profile.

In calculating segment lengths, when you divide circumference by number of segments, your given measurement is an arc length (a curved measurement) of the circumference curve. It's not quite the same thing as the length of a segment, which should be thought of as a chord length (a straight measurement). This difference can usually be ignored. It rarely makes a difference because a little extra thickness is generally added to the required diameters and to the width of the segments during the design process.If you consistently ignore this difference throughout the entire shape, everything should line up just fine. I only mention it for the math whiz who might question my calculation method.

Using Graph Paper

Computers are powerful tools, but they are not necessary for creating quality designs. A pencil with a good eraser, some graph paper, and a ruler are all you need. First, decide on the overall size of your turning. If it is bigger than your graph paper sheet, then you can tape multiple sheets together or you can work at a smaller scale. I personally like working with actual-size drawings. Since you do not have the ability to stretch or shrink the pencil drawing of your shape, as you can in a computer program, you might want to first calculate the total height of all your components (rings, feature ring, etc). As an example, imagine a vessel with these components:

• a bottom ring 1/2 inch high, .50;

• three main body rings each 3/4 inch high, 2.25;

• a feature ring 2 inch high, 2.00;

• two more body rings at 3/4 inch high, 1.50;

• a top ring that is 1/4 inch high, .25.

• Vessel height = 6.50 inches

By calculating the height first, you have avoided having to alter your component heights after you have determined the overall shape. If you prefer a vessel taller or shorter, then it is a matter of adding or deleting rings, or of changing ring heights. Next, you need to decide on the approximate diameter and shape for

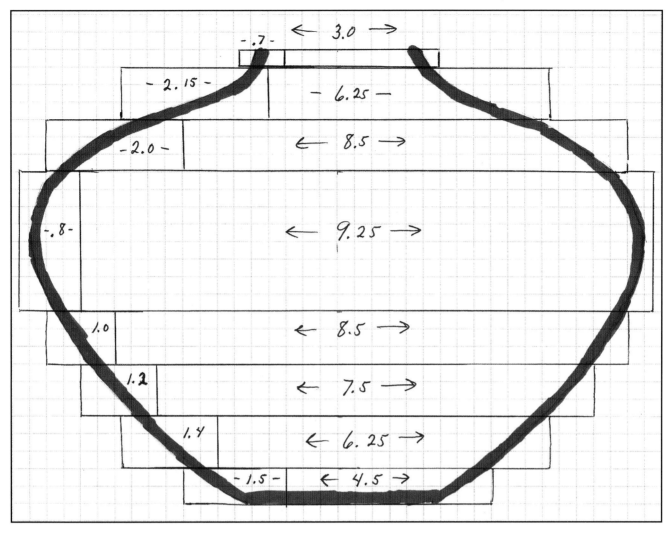

8-11   Using graph paper makes drawing a design much easier

your vessel. Mark on your graph paper the base and top elevations. Also, make a few reference marks so you know the location and diameter of your feature ring. It is likely to be the largest diameter ring, usually positioned at a point of profile transition. Then draw a few curved lines representing the vessel profile (**photo 8-11**). For now, focus on just one side of the vessel centerline. Play around with the profile until you are happy with the shape. Transfer the vessel profile to the other side by making a few corresponding pencil marks from the centerline, or by folding the paper down the centerline. Study the shape once again and repeat the process as many times as necessary. Now, thicken your outline to represent the wall thickness. Next, overlay onto the vessel profile a series of rectangles that represent the side

views of the individual rings. To provide a little room for error, draw these rectangles slightly wider than the diameter of the vessel. Measuring the length of these rectangles will give you the individual diameters of each ring. Next, overlay another series of smaller rectangles starting on the outside and going to the inside, to encompass the vessel wall thickness. Again, give yourself a little extra wood for errors. These smaller rectangles represent the individual segment widths in each ring or layer, that is, the width of the board from which you cut the segments. Now, all you need is the individual length of the segments in each ring. To determine the segment lengths, multiply the ring diameters by pi (3.1416) and then divide by the number of segments per ring. **Photo 8-11** shows a simple drawing using the previously listed ring heights. Though nothing fancy, it provides all the information needed.

If you are familiar with the computer spreadsheet program Excel and you are designing a large turning with many layers, then it is very simple to create a cutting list. The program formulas can do the math for you. Otherwise, just grab a calculator and manually do the math for each ring.

Using a CAD Program

Instead of using graph paper, the same design can be quickly developed using a computer drawing program. Using a computer doesn't mean your vessel design need be any different, it's just faster and more accurate. Using a computer also allows easily changing your design until you are completely satisfied. Years ago when I first became interested in segmented work, I was fortunate to already possess some CAD drawing experience, so it was just natural that I started creating my blueprints on a computer. I still use a very old Macintosh Classic computer with an ancient program called Claris CAD. People are amazed when they see this old relic still operating, but it works great and has all the power and features that I need; I will mourn its eventual demise. On a computer, you can draw a profile and manipulate the shape until you are satisfied — you do not have to keep erasing pencil lines to start over. In addition, the computer is very effective at smoothing your lines and transforming them into pleasing curves. The benefits of a computer-generated drawing are two-fold: it allows easy development of the turning's shape, and it provides you with all the dimensions you need for constructing and assembling your piece.

When using a computer program, the steps are not much different from paper and pencil. Shape comes first, followed by an overlay of rectangles in order to calculate dimensions. The computer is a major time saver and because it is so flexible, it enables you to focus on the form of your turning. Saved files can be recalled, modified, and then reused. I would be severely handicapped without the advantages of computer-aided design.

Specialized Computer Programs

Within the past few years several computer savvy woodturners have created commercially available programs that make the chore of designing a segmented turning very easy. It would be unfair of me to endorse one program over another, I really have not had the necessary experience with them to judge their differences. Quite frankly, because of my old Mac computer and CAD program, I do not need additional computer help. I will say that the limited experience that I have had with these new programs is very positive, and I definitely think they are great tools for woodturners. The programs are well worth the investment. They have their limitations — they are not CAD programs, meaning they will not allow you to draw out complex design elements, but with a minimum of learning time, one can quickly produce perfect lines and useful cutting lists.

A Sample Drawing

The most effective way to explain the complete design and construction process is to document the creation of a vessel. This is probably the next best thing to being in the shop with me. A friend, John, who provided me with some preferences, commissioned the vessel that I will make. He desired a 10-inch to 12-inch diameter Indian pot shape, he liked the look of what I call an Indian Blanket feature ring, and he really liked bubinga as the main wood. John also wanted something that would be stable on a coffee table in case it was bumped into from time to time. He liked one of my vessels that was on display at a local gallery, but he wanted it wider and shorter. What you will see is what he gets. Since John had a hand in the design process and since he is paying for it, I will refer to this piece as *JOHN'S TURNING*. Based on my conversation with John, I have drawn a rough sketch of the shape (**photo 8-12**).

At this point I know the components, but I have not decided the exact dimensions. I begin by thinking about this particular design and say,

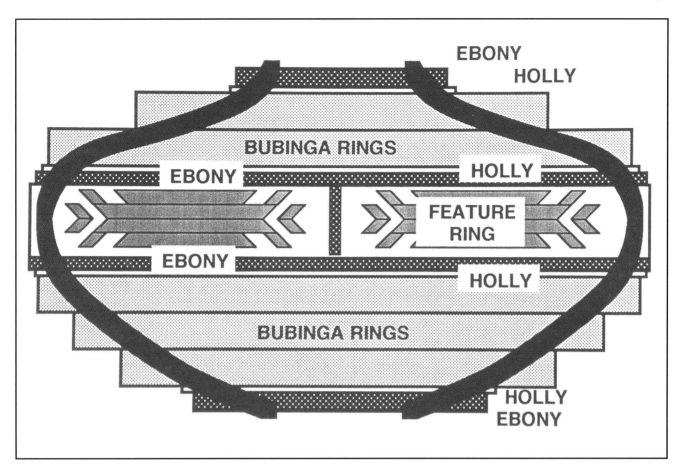

8-12   Computer drawing programs are very handy, but not necessary.

"Where do I want to start?" The most complex component is the feature ring with the Indian blanket-style geometric design. The exact final dimensions of the vessel are not critical, so why not construct the feature ring first? In the next chapter I will build the feature ring, finalize the vessel design and dimensions, and build this turning.

9-00   *JOHN'S TURNING* (12-1/2 inches diameter)— a lot of work, but worth the effort.

9-01   This is the feature ring for *JOHN'S TURNING.*

9.

John's Turning

The feature ring in *JOHN'S TURNING* is the focal point of the vessel. Indian blanket designs are very popular with the buying public and they are not nearly as difficult to construct as most people would guess. They do, however, require many accurately executed steps. While the feature ring may contain many individual pieces of wood, it's not necessary to individually cut every piece of wood. Follow along and you will see what I mean. **Photo 9-01** shows the completed feature ring that will be incorporated into *JOHN'S TURNING*.

Building an Indian Blanket Feature Ring

From an instructional point of view, it might seem strange to start out with the most complex step in this vessel's construction, but once you understand this process, the remainder of the project will seem simple. I chose bloodwood and holly as the two contrasting colors in this design element. This combination creates a dramatic contrast. However, it is a difficult combination for several reasons. The woods are of different densities, which presents a minor turning difficulty. Holly is so white in color that glue lines are difficult to hide. Bloodwood can stain the whiteness of the holly, and bloodwood is an oily, difficult wood to sand that gums up sandpaper very quickly. Having said all that, I still like the combination for its look, so it was worth the trouble. Here is my step-by-step procedure for constructing an Indian blanket feature ring:

First, I planed the bloodwood and holly boards to the same thickness of .9 inch. Using a table saw, I ripped strips 1.3 inch wide from each type of wood and ripped thin strips about 1/8 inch thick from the same boards. Ripping thin strips

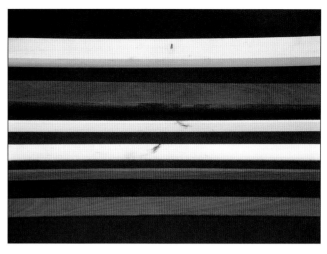

9-02 Accurate dimensioning of boards is essential.

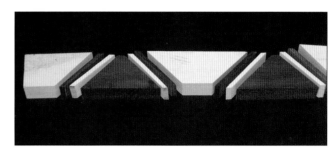

9-03 This is the arrangement of components prior to gluing.

is discussed in Chapter 7; a few of these strips can be seen in **photo 9-02**. One advantage of segmented work is, we do not require perfect boards. Defects such as the ones shown in the holly strips are easily worked around, discarded, and not a problem.

Using a miter saw set at 45°, I cut polygon-shaped pieces from the 1.3 inch wide strips. The point-to-point length of the holly pieces was not critical, though I did need about an inch of length on the short side. I cut the bloodwood pieces with their short sides less than a quarter-inch long. I have arranged a few of these components in **photo 9-03** to show you how I intended to glue them together.

The thin 1/8-inch wide strips were passed through a drum sander, erasing all saw blade marks and ensuring consistent thickness. I banded them together with masking tape, then gang cut them (at 45°) to lengths equal to the diagonal side of the polygons. I needed one

9-04   Anchor the first piece in the gluing jig.

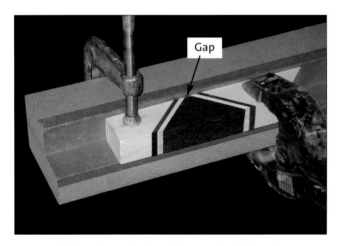

9-05   Prior to applying glue, a dry fit is always a good idea.

9-06   Accurate clamping is critical to success.

piece of each type of wood for each side of the bloodwood pieces; therefore, I cut 56 small strips of each color, plus a few extra in case I discovered a defective piece while gluing. A few of these thin, short strips are also shown in **photo 9-03**.

In this feature ring I decided to place 10 design elements around the vessel, as shown in **photo 9-01**. Each piece of bloodwood will produce one-half of a completed element, so I needed at least 20 pieces of bloodwood. This will become much clearer in the next few steps. I always make a few extra elements, so I will be able to reject a few after completion. With this in mind, I cut 28 pieces of bloodwood and 28 pieces of holly. Then I cut four of the holly pieces in half so that half-pieces could be positioned at each end of the strips that would be glued together later. This was enough pieces for 14 complete designs.

Since I had 28 pieces of bloodwood, I glued together four strips consisting of seven bloodwood pieces each. The gluing of these strips was perhaps the trickiest step in the construction. I used a simple gluing tray (**photo 9-04**) consisting of two strips of 1-inch MDF glued together to form a straight right-angle channel. I covered the jig with blue masking tape to allow removal of the strips after the glue had set for 30 to 40 minutes. Titebond was my glue choice. It was important that the bottom shelf of the gluing jig be slightly narrower than the polygons, so it would not interfere with the clamps. This meant the tray bottom was slightly less than 1.3 inch. **Photo 9-04** shows the gluing tray is slightly narrower than the holly strips.

To glue all these components together I used a C-clamp to firmly anchor a half-piece of the holly at the left end of the jig, with its long side against the backstop (**photo 9-04**). Then I gathered two thin bloodwood strips, two thin holly strips, one bloodwood polygon, and one holly polygon. Before applying glue I made sure that the surfaces were clean and free of any debris, and did a dry fit as shown in **photo 9-05**. I then clamped the piece of holly with a spring clamp and positioned it with a slight gap between the short side of the bloodwood piece and the back of the tray. This gap would be closed during the actual gluing step that follows.

I placed these pieces on the gluing tray with glue spread on all mating surfaces. With the spring clamp holding the holly piece in place I added a quick clamp to force the bloodwood piece against the back, which in turn forced the holly piece to slide slightly to the right while being resisted by the spring clamp. Done properly, there should be enough pressure on all the glue joints to ensure tight seams. If I have

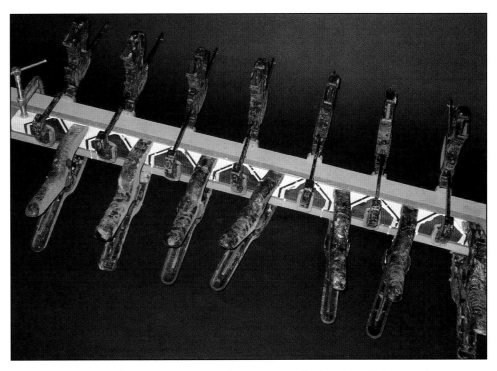

9-07   Here are the components of one strip all glued and clamped.

forced the piece of holly too far away, thereby causing a loose glue joint, I release the bloodwood clamp and force the holly piece back to the left, then attempt it again. It does require a little practice. Accurately gluing these pieces is critical to the creation of the completed design. The location of the center piece of bloodwood is especially important. It must be consistently and firmly seated against the back fence of the jig. If there is any gap, the components that are later cut will not be consistent in length.

This process was repeated, going from left to right, until all the pieces had been glued into four separate strips. One of the glued strips is shown in **photo 9-07**.

These four strips were quite fragile, so I cautiously used a chisel to pry them from the gluing tray. Using wax paper instead of masking tape on the gluing jig would have allowed easier removal of the strips, but it would not have provided enough resistance during the gluing process, the holly piece might have slid too easily away and the joints would not have been tight. Before the next cutting step, these strips were cleaned up. You can do it with a little handwork followed by light passes through a planer using a

9-08   To rip-cut thin strips, attach the board to a wider push board.

backing board. Once prepared, the strips could be smoothly rip-cut on the table saw. **Photo 9-08** shows ripping one of the cleaned-up strips attached to a wider push board of maple.

These glued strips were cut into four 1/8-inch thick strips using the technique described in Chapter 7. The exact thickness is not critical, but they must all be the same and it is extremely important to keep each set together. **Photo 9-09** shows one set of four strips in the

9-09   In this example, four strips were cut from each assembly.

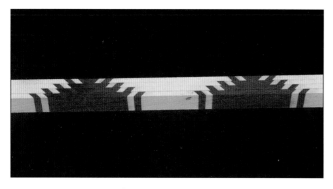

9-10   To create the desired design, each strip is flipped over.

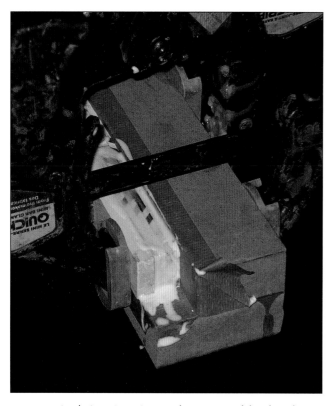

9-11   A gluing tray is used to assemble the thin strips.

order they were cut. The gaps represent the saw kerfs.

Flipping these strips over and reassembling them creates one-half of the design. The result of flipping the strips is shown in **photo 9-10**. The flip seems to confuse some people: each individual strip is flipped, not the stack as a unit.

Before gluing the strips together I passed them through the drum sander to erase all saw blade marks and to ensure tight glue lines. I was especially concerned with the appearance of the holly-to-holly glue lines. It was important to drum-sand off equal amounts from each of the strips, to accurately maintain the design and consistent thickness.

Centering all the strip elements with respect to each other would be difficult to do one at a time, but because of the way they were created it was quite easy. By accurately aligning the ends of each strip with one another, all the elements within the strip automatically lined up with each other. Even if one of the components was misaligned during the first gluing operation, everything must still line up now. You might have one unusable component, but the rest will be unaffected. **Photo 9-11** shows the ends of one grouping, glued together and clamped using the same gluing tray as the first glue job. I did have to rip the gluing tray down to accommodate the narrower assembly. In addition to the four thin strips I have added a thicker strip of holly, which will become the top and bottom border around the blanket design. Glue obscures the view, but the four thin strips near the end of the gluing tray are perfectly aligned with each other. If the ends of these thin strips are not accurately aligned, then every design element will also be out of alignment.

Using a combination of a hand plane, the drum sander, and the table saw, I cleaned up these four new strips.

Using a miter saw at 90°, I separated the strips into individual pieces. These cuts did not have to be exact, I just eyeballed the center between the designs. Each piece represents one-half of a design element. **Photo 9-12** shows the miter saw separating the components.

These half-pieces were carefully paired before being glued together. If two halves did not quite match perfectly, I put one aside and tried another. By trial and error and a little adjustment using the disc sander, I managed to match all the half-pieces; a few unglued pairs are shown in **photo 9-13**. Inaccurate alignment of the two halves is easily noticed, so I took extreme care while gluing.

Even though I only needed 10 completed elements, I glued all the halves together because a few were not likely to pass muster and at this point it is far too late to go back and make more. **Photo 9-14** shows two halves clamped together to form one complete design.

I cleaned up the completed designs on the disc sander and inspected them once more. By checking both sides, I was able to select the 10 best. These elements now needed to be miter-cut in order to form the 360° ring: 10 pieces, 20 angles, therefore, 18° per end.

Centering the bloodwood between the miter cuts is important. By placing one side of a square even with the end of the longest bloodwood piece, I made a pencil mark on each segment. These marks were then aligned with a mark on my saw bed and one end was miter-cut off all the segments (**photo 9-15**). Then, using a stop block carefully positioned to center the bloodwood shapes, I cut the other ends. I intentionally cut these segments a little long, which allowed me to check the fit and to check the centering of the bloodwood within the holly. I readjusted my miter saw stop block to remove a tiny bit of length from the segments then re-cut whichever end appeared longer, thereby improving the centering of the bloodwood. I repeated this process once again in order to get every component as centered as possible, while maintaining equal segment lengths.

The width of the segments (from outside to inside) left little room for error, the ring had to be perfectly round. In cases such as this, a

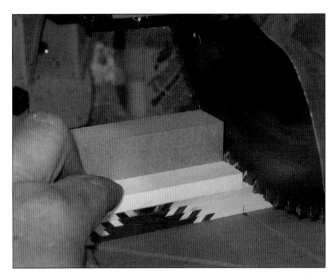

9-12 A miter saw is used to cut individual half-components.

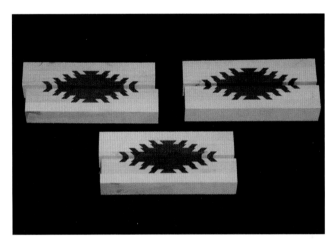

9-13 The half-components must match perfectly.

9-14 Precise alignment during gluing is essential.

9-15   The miter saw is used to create segments from the glued assemblies.

9-16   Splines are cut with the same horizontal grain orientation.

9-17   Good planning ensures a successful glue job.

sanding jig is necessary. Sanding jig construction and use is discussed in Chapter 7. I lightly sanded the ends, assembled the ring using a hose clamp, and checked the fit against a bright light. The joints have to be perfect to the naked eye when dry-clamped and held up to a bright light.

My design called for a vertical piece of ebony positioned between each element. Perhaps it would have been easier to cut short pieces of ebony from a long strip, but that would have positioned the ebony grain perpendicular to the grain of the blanket segments. Instead, I cut them using the miter saw at 90°, orienting the grain horizontally to match the holly and bloodwood (**photo 9-16**). Notice the shape of the segment hold-down device. Another example of maintaining consistent grain orientation is shown in **photo 5-03**. In general, I try to avoid any glue lines with perpendicular grain longer than about 3/4 inch. I decided that 1/4-inch wide pieces of ebony would look right. These parallel-sided pieces of ebony had no effect on the fit of the miter joints. Instead of using the disc sander, I just made a few light swirling passes by hand on a piece of 80-grit paper adhered to a flat piece of MDF before the gluing step.

Gluing the final assembly was the easiest step. I decided to glue the entire ring at one time. I wanted to accomplish this quickly so I gathered up everything I needed before starting (**photo 9-17**). During gluing, the key things to pay attention to are: all surfaces clean, all surfaces receive glue, all corners meet evenly, and all segments sit flush with one another. A clean gluing environment is important, so I usually use my shop vac to blow off shavings and dust from my arms and clothing, which minimizes the risk of debris falling into the glue joints. I applied glue quickly and liberally to both ends of each segment and to both sides of each piece of ebony. It is critical that all the outside corners line up just as they did during the dry-fit inspection. It is also important that the tops and bottoms of all the parts remain flush with one another. A few light taps with a hammer before final clamp tightening is usually sufficient. I ran a finger around the top surface to make sure everything

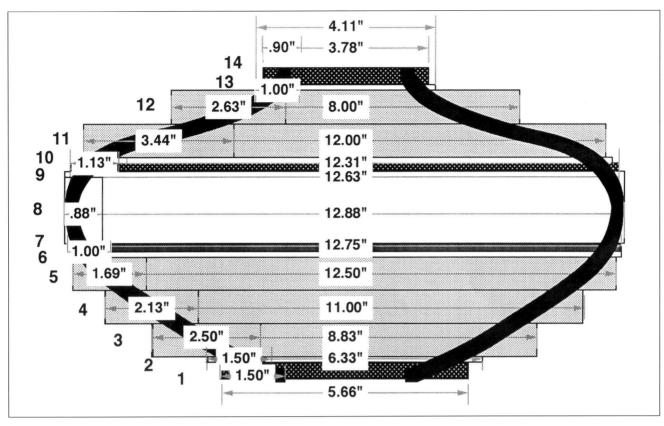

9-18   After building the feature ring, final dimensions can be determined.

was flush. Wiping excess glue off the surface with a small scrap of wood is another way to double-check the evenness of the surface.

The technique for constructing this feature ring (**photo 9-01**) can be easily altered to create bigger, smaller, simpler, or more complex Indian blanket designs. It is an easy way to make very complex-looking designs, containing hundreds of pieces of wood that do not require individual handling. This feature ring contains 590 individual pieces of wood, but as you can now see, I did not individually cut and glue 590 pieces.

Now, back to *JOHN'S TURNING*. The finished feature ring measured 12.8 inches in diameter. Using that information, I adjusted the original turning design and created my final blueprint (**photo 9-18**). During the construction description that follows, I make many references to the various numbered rings layers; these numbers appear on the left side of the drawing. The original drawing was done actual size but here has been reduced to fit the page size. When creating such a drawing, first focus

on the shape. Once you are satisfied, add the rectangles that represent the rings and segments. The little bit of extra rectangle length that you provide here will give you latitude as you construct and shape the vessel profile.

Using the measurements from this blueprint, I created a cutting list (next page) that would be very handy in the shop while constructing the ring layers. I created this list on a computer using the spreadsheet program Excel, but a small calculator certainly would have worked.

The list contains all the information I needed to construct the turning. The highlighted segment-length column is probably the most critical and requires the most attention during the cutting. If using a calculator, just multiply the ring diameters by pi (3.1416) and then divide by the number of segments. The figures in the board length column are simply segment lengths times number of segments. No allowance is added for saw kerf loss because the angle of the miter cut usually offsets it. Having this checklist in the shop was invaluable.

Cutting List for *John's Turning*

Ring Number	Ring Diameter*	Miter Angle	Number of Segments	Width of Segments*	Height of Segments*	Length of Segments*	Wood Type	Board Length**
1	5.66	18°	10	1.50	0.40	1.78	ebony	18
2	6.33	18°	10	1.50	0.13	1.99	holly	20
3	8.83	9°	20	2.50	0.80	1.39	bubinga	28
4	11.00	9°	20	2.13	0.80	1.73	bubinga	35
5	12.50	9°	20	1.69	0.80	1.96	bubinga	39
6	12.75	9°	20	1.00	0.13	2.00	holly	40
7	12.75	9°	20	1.00	0.19	2.00	ebony	40
FEATURE	12.88	18°	10	0.88	1.63	n/a	n/a	n/a
9	12.63	9°	20	1.29	0.19	1.98	ebony	40
10	12.31	9°	20	1.29	0.13	1.93	holly	39
11	12.00	9°	20	3.44	0.80	1.89	bubinga	38
12	8.00	9°	20	2.63	0.80	1.26	bubinga	25
13	4.11	18°	10	1.00	0.13	1.29	holly	13
14	3.78	18°	10	0.90	0.40	1.19	ebony	12

* all figures represent inches

**rough estimate based on the length of segments times the number of segments

The feature-ring construction was the most difficult part of this project. The rest was simply a matter of building and stacking segment rings. Because of the shape of the vessel, internal turning would be difficult if the shape were created one layer at a time starting at the base. For this reason, and because working in two directions is more efficient, I built the top and bottom separately and then joined the two halves. I started by constructing the bottom and top rings of ebony. Using the cutting list, I cut the ebony segments using the miter saw (the table saw would have worked as well).

The top and bottom ebony rings were small and absolute roundness was not critical. Therefore I sanded the segment-ends freehand, without a sanding jig. Gluing all the segments at once was a little risky. I preferred either of the other two methods, rub joint or half-ring. I glued these rings using the rub-joint technique of joining pairs. **Photo 9-19** shows the second step of gluing together the top and bottom ebony rings.

The base ring needed a plug in the bottom of the vessel. I chose a piece of holly and used the technique described in Chapter 7 to create a good fit between the plug and ebony ring. Plugs require very little clamping pressure to be held in place — a spare faceplate or similar weight is more than enough.

After the plug-joint had cured, I turned the surface that would be the bottom of the vessel flat and smooth. I then removed this base ring with its plug and permanently glued it (Titebond) to another faceplate and waste block that had been turned to the same diameter, making it easy to center. Perhaps this all sounds a little complicated, but it is really quite simple and quickly accomplished. **Photo 9-20** shows the top and bottom ebony rings ready for attachment to additional vessel rings.

I flattened the ebony rings so they were ready for the attachment of the adjoining holly rings. Even though the two finished holly rings needed to be only .125 inch tall, I glued them up from .375-inch thick material. This was easier to handle and easy to turn down to the final thickness after attachment to the ebony rings. I temporarily attached the holly rings to small waste blocks that would act as handles, and flattened them on one side using the disc sander. Using a clamp from the ceiling, I then glued them to the ebony rings.

The order of constructing the remaining rings made little difference. However, to save wood it is best to rip the widest segment material first. After I cut the wide segments, I was able to re-rip the unused portion of those strips to the next widest dimension. If I had started with the narrowest strips of wood first, then I would have been unable to use leftovers for the wider segments. I continued to build the bubinga rings in the order of width, from widest to narrowest. My bubinga strips were all cut from the same wide board, thus ensuring similar coloring. If several boards of varying color had been used, then I would have mixed up the arrangement of segments by randomly cutting strips from different boards.

Before completing the construction of the remaining bubinga rings, I prepared the base of the turning for its first bubinga ring. The holly ring was turned down to its designed thickness (.125 inch) and I finalized the gluing surface using a sanding block.

Ring #3 was attached with hot-melt onto a faceplate-mounted centering board. Using concentric pencil circles, the bubinga ring was centered by eyeballing its outside edges. If you distrust your eyeballing capabilities, then use a caliper to center the ring as shown in **photo 9-21**.

When joining the holly ring to the first bubinga ring, only the portion of the bubinga ring that contacted the holly needed flattening. The portion of bubinga that extended beyond the holly was turned down below the glue surface, thus allowing me to focus on the glue joint. In **photo 9-22** (next page), ring #3 has been flattened and cleaned with canned air. The surface can be cleaned with compressed air if you have it, or with the exhaust port of a shop vacuum. For small dusting jobs, canned air is effective and convenient. You can sometimes find three-packs, reasonably priced, at the large warehouse-type stores.

9-19   Construction starts with both top and bottom ebony rings.

9-20   Top and bottom rings are secured to faceplates.

9-21   Precise centering of rings is important.

9-22   Clean surfaces help ensure good glue joints.

9-23   Initially, keep the vessel walls at maximum thickness.

Once this flattening process was completed I glued the two rings together using the lathe as my clamp and centering device. My tailstock live-center just happens to fit very nicely into the threaded recess of my faceplates. **Photo 7-30** in Chapter 7 shows the procedure.

I added rings #4 and #5 just as ring #3 had been prepared and glued. I also added rings #12 and then #11 to the top of the vessel. While preparing the glue surfaces I also did a little rough turning on the inside and outside of the vessel. I only removed wood that I was certain would have to be removed later, as shown in **photo 9-23**. I maintained a majority of the possible wall thickness until most of the vessel had been constructed. Retaining maximum wall thickness gave me options during the final shaping.

There were several ways to put together rings #6 through #10. There are many steps involved and it can get confusing. Here is how I did it. Since rings #6 and #10 are thin layers of holly about the same diameter, I cut, sanded, and glued together (using the half-ring method) one thicker holly ring. I also did the same for ebony rings #7 and #9. I then lightly attached the ebony ring to a round piece of particleboard using a few beads of hot melt glue. The particleboard provided a handle for holding the ring against my disc sander to flatten and

smooth one side. I could have done this on the lathe, but my sander is big enough and I was not concerned about turning the ebony ring round at this stage.

I flattened the feature ring using the disc sander and then glued the ebony ring to it using many spring clamps (this is shown in Chapter 7, **photo 7-29**). I flattened the holly ring on the disc sander same as the ebony ring. Then I glued it to ring #5, clamping with a pipe clamp that pushes from my shop ceiling. I have many different length pipes and I use this technique quite often, because it does not tie up my lathe. This holly ring is fairly sturdy, but just as with thinner and weaker rings I positioned it on a thin layer of rubber mat that was covered with wax paper. The rubber router pad supports the ring very evenly, helping to distribute the clamping pressure.

In **photo 9-24**, the bottom of the turning with the holly ring has been lathe-mounted. The exposed side of the holly has been flattened and the upper portion of the turning has been glued onto the holly ring using the tailstock as a clamp.

After the glue cured, I parted the holly ring in half as shown in **photo 9-25**. I then turned down the holly rings (rings #6 & #10) to a thickness of about 1/8 inch and flattened the gluing surfaces. These two halves of the

9-24 Planning ahead can save assembly steps.

9-25 Splitting a ring results in a two-for-one benefit.

9-26 Here is another example of two-from-one ring usage.

9-27 Masking tape can be being used as a positioning aid.

turning were then set aside.

I mounted (again using hot-melt) the feature ring with the ebony ring to my centering faceplate. I flattened the exposed surface of the ebony ring, and as you can see in **photo 9-26**, I glued the upper portion of the turning to the ebony ring.

I parted the ebony ring into two rings as I had done with the holly ring, and turned down the two ebony rings to a height of approximately 3/16 inch. When the vessel is shaped, the angle of exposure will make this 3/16 inch ring appear a little thicker, closely matching the 1/4-inch wide vertical pieces of ebony in the feature ring.

In **photo 9-27**, I have removed the feature ring from the centering plate and I have carefully centered and glued to it to the base of the turning using the ceiling clamp system. At this point I have assembled the entire turning into two halves and both pieces are still mounted and centered on their original faceplates.

Now it is a matter of turning the outside profiles to their final shape. A frequent visual check of the outside profile is necessary during the outside shaping — the line has to be just right. The outside profile can be turned with the two halves temporarily joined using a little double-sided tape plus support from the tailstock. In this case I simply held the two

9-28   Finish-sand the inside prior to joining the two halves.

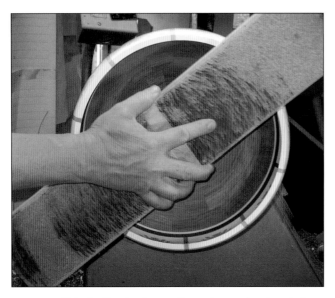

9-29   This is the last sanding step prior to gluing the halves together.

9-30   Take steps to minimize glue squeeze-out contamination.

halves together frequently, to examine the profile as I finalized the shape. I carefully matched the inside and outside diameters of the mating surfaces and turned the insides of the two halves to their final wall thickness. In this particular vessel, I was striving for a consistent wall of 3/16 inch. If the vessel had been much smaller, my thickness goal would have been closer to 1/8 inch. While it certainly would have been possible to turn the wall down thinner, based on my conversation with its owner I wanted the vessel to be able to survive a fall to the floor.

The vessel's top opening was too small for my hand, so it only made sense to sand the inside as much as possible before gluing the two halves together. Both insides were power-sanded to 400-grit (**photo 9-28**) and both mating surfaces received one last touch of the sanding block (**photo 9-29**). I also checked the matching diameters one last time.

I did not want the difficult task of cleaning up any glue squeeze-out that might run down the inside surface. I used masking tape to create a barrier, as shown in **photo 9-30**.

Joining Two Halves

The big moment had finally come. I glued the two halves together as shown in **photo 9-31**. I predetermined the rotational alignment and positioned a piece of masking tape, which I then cut at the glue joint line. The tape gives me quick rotational alignment, allowing me to focus on the critical centering of the two pieces. Usually the diameters are not a 100% match, creating a tiny ridge. Using my fingernails, I can judge the consistency of this tiny ridge all around the circumference and make slight adjustments as necessary. The clamping pressure in this case is simply a few faceplates, about 15 pounds. The total surface area of the glue joint is quite small and does not require a lot of pressure. I did not use the ceiling clamp because I did not want the distraction of having to adjust the angle of pressure, which otherwise might force the upper portion to slip sideways. Stacked weights provide enough centered force.

9-31   Concentric alignment of the two halves is critical.

I try to time this step so the glue can cure overnight, for two reasons: I want a strong glue joint prior to continuing, and I want any glue squeeze-out on the inside to be dry so that when the vessel is spun, the squeeze-out does not smear.

The next morning I mounted the vessel using the top faceplate (**photo 9-32**). The glue job had perfectly centered the two halves, making it possible to turn the vessel from either faceplate. This made it easy to finish the base shaping without the interference of the lathe headstock — not a big deal, but having the vessel positioned this way did help.

After using a 1/2-inch bowl gouge and a 1-inch shear scraper, I made a few passes with a hand-held cabinet scraper (**photo 9-33**). My goal with these tools was to create a surface that did not require coarse sanding. I wanted to start sanding with 180-grit, because with

9-32   A perfect glue job allows lathe mounting from either end.

9-33   Before sanding, a fine burr on a cabinet scraper can improve the surface quality.

80-grit, the combination of soft holly and hard ebony would be easy to over-sand, creating an uneven surface.

The Finishing Process

After completing the base I re-mounted the vessel using the base faceplate, removed the top faceplate, and turned off the waste block. I finish-turned the upper half of the vessel and power-sanded its entire surface to 400-grit. I cleaned up the inside glue joint with a hook-

9-34   My wife's small hands are invaluable.

9-35   This is an effective method of reverse mounting the vessel.

shaped Stewart scraping tool. All surfaces were then cleaned with a tack cloth and made ready for the first of two coats of sanding sealer. The top opening, as I knew it would be, was far too small for my hand to enter. **Photo 9-34** reveals one of my secret tools — a willing, enthusiastic wife with small hands. Without Tere's assistance, I would have been fumbling

with a rag on a stick for who knows how long. It is just as important to protect the inside as the outside. The finish is a barrier against moisture. To prevent unequal wood movement, both sides need the same treatment. If a vessel opening is too small for anyone's hand, then the next best thing is to pour oil in, swirl it around, drain it back out, and wipe it dry as best you can with a rag attached to a dowel.

After drying for 24 hours, the vessel was sanded again with 400-grit and rubbed with super-fine steel wool, preparing it for the second coat of sanding sealer. The final finish was four coats, applied one each day, of a satin tung oil/urethane product made by General Finishes (the green can). Before applying each finish coat, I rubbed down the surface with steel wool and cleaned it with a tack cloth. After the final coat, I buffed the surface with a polishing compound using a buffing disc mounted in a hand drill. I did all the finishing and final buffing with the vessel still mounted on the base faceplate.

I prefer non-glossy finishes. I want the wood to look and feel like wood, not plastic, although, I have to say, I have seen some very professional glossy finishes on turnings. Sometimes I have put a shine on a piece by applying a final coat of buffed wax, but it is not my most-used finish. A satin sheen is just my personal preference.

We are almost done. With a vessel this size, I partially part off the waste block and then finish the job with the band saw. If you have ever cut something round on a band saw, then you know it can be tricky. The saw teeth will try to rotate the turning in your hands. Be careful if you attempt this — keep your hands clear and maintain a firm grip as you cut slowly. If this procedure makes you nervous, then do not try it. There are other ways to remove the base block. A handsaw while the piece is still on the lathe is one way. Reverse-mounting the vessel and turning off the block is another. My most common method of reverse-mounting is to cut a recessed groove into a mounted piece of MDF to snugly fit the vessel top, and then attach a donut-shaped ring of MDF using 5/16-inch all-thread rods. Thin layers of foam rubber and pieces of paper towel protect the vessel finish, as shown in **photo 9-35**.

I'm not sure why, but one of the first things people do after they pick up a woodturning is look at the bottom, so I try to give them a little something to look at. To create a professional looking bottom, I reverse-mount the vessel, turn, sand, and sign the bottom before applying finish. If there is room, I usually record the wood species used. My choice for any writing work is a simple wood burning tool. It may seem like an insignificant detail, but people will look at your signature with great interest, so it pays to design and execute it with great care. I usually try to include a white piece of wood in the base, just to have a good surface upon which to burn (**photo 9-36**). Even if you are not selling to the public, your family and heirs will appreciate the signature. If your design requires dark-colored wood on the bottom, then use a silver or white fine-tipped permanent marking pen. Do not remove the vessel from the reverse-mounting device until you have finished signing the bottom. If you remove it before signing, and happen to mess up with the wood burner, then you will have to go through the mounting process again. If it is still mounted, it is relatively simple to turn off the mistake and redo the signing. Hurray, we are done with this one!

In the world of segmented turning, this vessel (**photo 9-00**, page 72) is a very typical design. You might be thinking, "This is too much work, I think I'll stick to big blocks of wood." Do not be discouraged that easily. While it is a lot of work, it can be very satisfying. If you give it a chance, many of the techniques that I have described will become almost second nature and you will quickly learn methods that significantly shorten construction time.

9-36   Always sign your work.

10-00 *CHESS PIECES* (tallest is 5-1/2 inches) are examples of forms built using small staves.

10-01   *THREE WEDDING GIFTS* (10 inches tall), hollow turnings constructed of staves.

10.

Stave Construction

While stacking rings is the most common way to construct a segmented turning, there is another technique: staves. Wooden barrels were built from staves hundreds of years ago. The wine industry still favors stave-constructed oak barrels for wine aging. There are two basic types of stave-constructed forms: one is built using simple miters, the other is constructed from staves with angled miters, known as compound miters. Simple miters are certainly easier to construct, they are just tall segments with the wood grain oriented vertically. However, they do not provide much opportunity for creating a non-parallel shape, unless the boards are quite thick. The chess pieces in **photo 10-00** are miniature examples of stave construction. Simple-mitered staves comprise the portions of the chess pieces with the dark veneer splines. Because of the small size (the king is 5.5 inches tall), there was no reason to use compound-mitered staves. In case you were wondering, the grain orientation of all the sections is vertical.

Compound miters make possible a wide range of vessel wall angles. Shapes can range from a very shallow dish to a vertical profile. By adjusting two angles, the saw blade angle and the miter gauge angle, we can achieve a variety of shapes. Calculating compound miter angles is more complicated than simple miters, it is not just a matter of dividing 360° by twice the number of segments. There are two key variables: the number of staves, and the slope angle of the desired form. The number of staves is simply your decision based upon stave width and vessel circumference. In other words, desired diameter multiplied by pi and divided by desired stave width, equals number of staves. The other variable, slope angle, is measured between the side of the form and the flat surface upon which it sits (assuming the form is cone-shaped with the small end at the base). A tall vessel would likely have a slope of more than 60°, whereas a shallow platter would probably have a slope of less than 25°. The slope is completely up to you to determine, use a protractor and draw a few lines to help you decide.

Calculating Compound Miter Angles

Do not worry, you do not have to go back to your high school geometry books. In the appendix of this book I have provided a chart listing the angles most commonly needed. However, if you need to determine a set of angles not listed in the provided chart, and you are not afraid of a little mathematics, then you will need a calculator with trig functions and the following formulas:

(If you have no interest in calculating compound miter angles, then skip ahead a few pages.)

Miter Angle (MA) = inverse tan (1 ÷ {cosS ∗ tan[360 ÷ (2N)]})

Blade Angle (BA) = inverse tan (cosMA ∗ tanS)

MA is the miter angle,

S is the slope of the vessel (measured from horizontal to side),

BA is the saw blade bevel angle,

N is the number of staves.

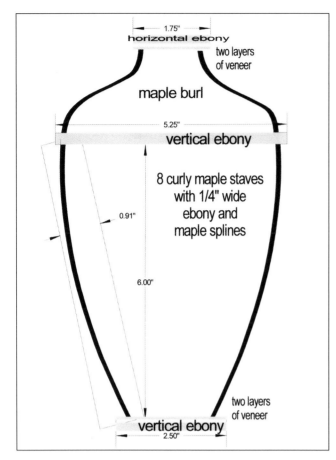

1.75"
horizontal ebony

two layers
of veneer

maple burl

5.25"
vertical ebony

8 curly maple staves
with 1/4" wide
ebony and
maple splines

0.91"

6.00"

two layers
of veneer

vertical ebony
2.50"

10-02   Staved vessels also require careful planning.

Trust me, this is easier than it looks. You do not have to understand cosines and tangents, you only need to know how to push the right buttons on a calculator that has those functions. Make sure the calculator is in degree mode, not radian mode. Start by first selecting two numbers, the number of staves and the slope of the vessel. I will take you through the process using 75° as the slope angle and 12 as the number of staves. The width of the staves has no bearing upon the angles, it is only varied to change the circumference (and diameter) of the form. Because the blade angle (BA) formula needs the miter angle (MA), I must calculate it first. Below I have inserted 75° as the slope and 12 as the number of staves.

Miter Angle (MA) = inverse tan (1 ÷ [cos75° * tan(360° ÷ (2*12))])

Using my calculator, I next determine the cosine of 75° to be .258819, I have done the math (360° ÷ (2*12)) which equals 15°, and I have calculated

the tangent of 15° as .2679491. Therefore:

Miter Angle (MA) = inverse tan (1 ÷ (.258819 * .2679491))

I continue by performing the multiplication

Miter Angle (MA) = inverse tan (1 ÷ .0693503)

and the division as shown above.

Miter Angle (MA) = inverse tan 14.419548

To convert the inverse tangent to degrees of angle, use the calculator once more. You might have an inverse button (INV) or, as on my calculator, hit shift-tan to display the inverse:

Miter Angle (MA) = 86.032872° or 86.03°

Now with the miter angle (MA) known, I can find the blade angle (BA). Below, I have put the miter angle and the slope angle in the formula.

Blade Angle (BA) = inverse tan(cos86.032872° * tan75°)

The calculator provides these figures:

Blade Angle (BA) = inverse tan(.0691841 * 3.7320508)

The multiplication results:

Blade Angle (BA) = inverse tan .2581985

The calculator converts the inverse of the blade angle tangent to the blade angle in degrees:

Blade Angle (BA) = 14.477495° or 14.48°

The next step is to adjust your saw to these angles (blade angle 14.48°, and miter angle 86.03°). I hope this is a little clearer than mud; it can certainly be confusing, especially if you do not use it very often. That is the convenience of charts, but if you ever have to calculate angles for a stave-constructed form not listed, now you know where to find the procedure.

Building A Staved Vessel
Staves cut with the grain positioned vertically present another problem if you desire to attach additional layers. Consistent grain orientation becomes difficult to maintain. I will show you how I deal with that problem as I build a stave-constructed vessel.

The first step, just as with the previous project (*JOHN'S TURNING*), is to develop a design. I looked over my wood inventory and decided to build three small vessels using narrow, 2-inch wide curly maple boards, cut-offs I purchased from a guitar blank supplier. Guitar suppliers secure some of the finest woods available and they sell some terrific looking scraps at reasonable prices. Based on my wood selection, I created a simple drawing (**photo 10-02**). I decided to build the stave portion of my three vessels using eight sides, with a slope angle of 75° (or 15° from vertical), and to use solid pieces of maple burl for the top shoulder section of the vessels. I needed wedding gifts for two of my nieces, so these vases were just the ticket.

Referring to the table of compound miter angles (page 176), I find that I need to cut my staves with a saw blade angle of 21.69° and a miter gauge angle of 83.88°. I wish it were that simple. Unless your equipment is a lot more high-tech than mine, setting up these angles requires trial and error. That's why I decided to build three similar vessels at the same time. After the lengthy process of adjusting my saw, I want to make more than one turning. The boards were narrow and about 22 inches long. I first machined them flat and straight using a jointer/planer, then crosscut them into 7-inch long rectangles. To cut these rectangles into staves, I used a shop-built sliding table saw sled that securely held the wood for consistently accurate cuts. **Photo 10-03** shows my sled device. It is made from 1-inch thick MDF with two runners on the bottom that fit quite snugly into my table saw miter gauge slots. This eliminates any side-to-side sloppiness in the travel as it is pushed into the saw blade. At the top of the photo, you will notice a bridge of 1-inch MDF spanning the two sides. It stabilizes the two sides of the sled by securely connecting them across the saw blade kerf. At the back of the sled is an adjustable 2-inch thick lamination of MDF that acts as a miter gauge.

This sled is similar to the miter-cutting sled described in Chapter 7, with adjustability for different angles and without the tapered exit ramp. Before setting up this sled to cut the

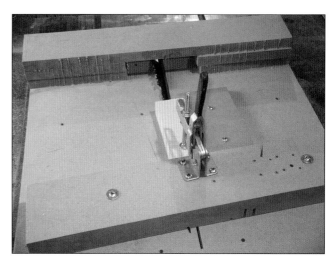

10-03 A table saw sled is used to cut compound miters.

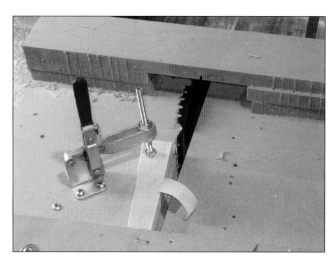

10-04 After cutting one side, set up the sled for the second sides.

compound miters, I cut 1-inch thick MDF into rectangles that matched my curly maple pieces, for making test cuts before sawing the good stuff. Using a protractor, I positioned the MDF miter gauge as closely as I could to 83.88°, realistically, to within 1° of that angle. Next, I adjusted my saw blade as close as possible to the desired 21.69°. For safety and accuracy's sake, I positioned a hold-down clamp on the sled to firmly secure the wood. If you look to the right side of the hold-down clamp, you can see a piece of MDF attached as backstop, thereby ensuring identically dimensioned pieces. The 1-inch thickness of the sled allows for easy, secure screw-attachment of components such as stop blocks and hold-down clamps.

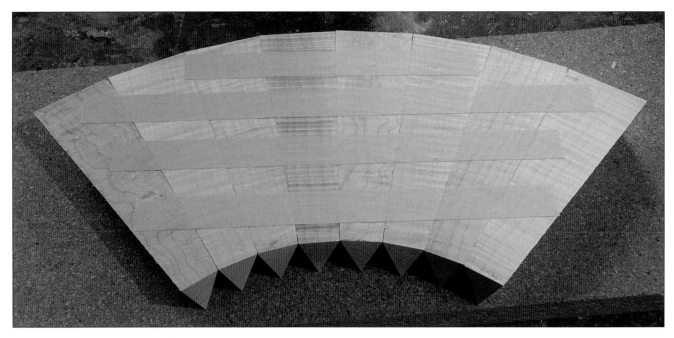

10-05   Checking the dry-fit is very important.

I first cut eight test pieces on one side. Then I crosscut a piece of MDF to create an angled stop block, which I attached to the other side of the blade. In **photo 10-04**, you can see this stop block with the hold-down clamp mounted on top of it. You will also notice a piece of tape attached to the piece of wood which is about to be cut. Because I have used this sled for many other projects, the kerf has become much wider than the blade, allowing narrow cut-offs to fall into the kerf and jam. By holding the end of the tape in one hand as I pushed the sled with the other, I could retrieve the cutoff before it caused a problem.

After cutting the other sides of the test pieces, I laid them out on a flat surface and taped them together much like the maple pieces in **photo 10-05**. I rolled the form into a cone shape and checked the accuracy of the angles. After the first test cuts I was only off a tiny bit. The angles were a little tight on the inside, causing a slight gap between the untaped outside edges. This meant I needed a tiny bit more angle on one of my settings. It is important to note that any time you vary from a given chart angle, you will also alter the slope of the form. I was not worried about achieving an exact 75° slope, because I had enough wood thickness for turning the desired profile. Therefore, I

proceeded by adjusting only one angle until the fit was right. Since I had screwed down the MDF miter gauge, it was much simpler to adjust the blade angle. After looking at the first test assembly, I estimated that I was off a total of approximately 2° or less. By dividing 2° by 16 (the number of angles), I determined that I only had to increase the blade angle by about .12°, which is not very much. I knew that my saw blade angle adjusting handle moves the blade 1.5° per revolution, so I had to turn the handle less than 1/8 of a revolution. This sounds like splitting hairs, but that is how I decided my next move.

You might be wondering how I estimated that my first set of cuts was off by approximately 2°. Since the circumference of any ring contains 360°, if a circumference were 360 inches, then each degree would span 1 inch. Likewise, if a circumference were 36 inches, then 1° would equal 1/10 inch (36 inches divided by 360°). The vessel under construction had a circumference of approximately 16 inches, therefore each degree equaled approximately .04 inch (16 inches divided by 360°). I estimated that the total width of gap on the outside of the first set of test pieces was less than .1 inch, therefore I needed to increase the total of all the angles by approximately 2° (.1 inch divided by .04 inch).

This type of estimating is rough, but it is better than haphazardly adjusting the saw blade.

I made the 1/8 of a turn adjustment and cut eight more test pieces, taped them together, and checked for accuracy once again. I was lucky, they fit perfectly; usually at least one more set of test pieces is required. I cut the first eight staves and checked the fit once again, using the tape-together technique shown in **photo 10-05**. After confirming the settings I cut the other 16 staves, giving me enough to glue together three different cone-shaped forms. No matter how many attempts it takes, the fit has to be near-perfect and if the form is to be glued together all at one time, then the fit has be absolutely perfect, at least to the naked eye.

Before gluing these staves together I needed to create a laminated spline, to glue between the staves. This was a five-piece lamination, as shown in **photo 10-06**, consisting of two pieces of maple veneer, two pieces of ebonized walnut veneer, and one piece of 1/8-inch thick ebony. To either side of the lamination components you can see a piece of 3/4-inch MDF covered with blue masking tape. These are cauls, to be placed on the outside of the laminations to provide uniform clamping pressure. I glued the layers of wood together, cleaned them up, and cut them to length. These splines had parallel sides, so they had no effect on the fit of the staves.

I then laid out the assembly of staves and splines flat (outside up) and applied tape to each seam. I paid special attention to make sure the tape was well adhered to the splines, so it would keep them in place during the gluing and clamping. When applying the tape, do not squeeze the pieces together tightly. The tape should not restrict the staves from easily folding in to form a circle. The tape is only an aid in the assembly process, not a clamp. After applying the tape, I used another board on top of the assembly to turn it outside down as shown in **photo 10-7**.

Gluing together compound miters is more difficult than gluing simple miters. Because of the angle of the outside profiles, hose clamps may slip and not provide the needed pressure.

10-06　The splines are a five-layer lamination.

10-07　The assembly is now ready for glue.

Depending upon the acuteness of the outside slope, rubber bands might not stay in place. Gluing these forms together presents challenges for which I will suggest a few solutions.

My preferred method of clamping this type of cone-shaped form requires constructing a customized gluing jig. To build this jig, I band-saw four circles of 3/4-inch MDF and mounted one to a faceplate. I then secured the other three to the mounted circle with a single centered screw, as shown in **photo 10-08** (next page). The circles were then all turned to the same diameter (this was not necessary, but it looked better than rough band-saw cuts). Before taking the circles apart I drilled three evenly spaced holes near the outside edge, to accommodate 5/16-inch all-thread rods used to clamp the

10-08   This will become a gluing jig for all-at-one-time stave gluing.

10-09   A parting tool is used to cut donut-shaped rings for the gluing jig.

10-10   This style of gluing jig requires perfect miter angles.

form. I also made reference marks in order to maintain the original alignment of the outside holes while gluing and clamping. This will make more sense in another couple of photos.

I took the assembly of circles apart and using the center holes I mounted each one onto a screw chuck as shown in **photo 10-09**.

Using a parting tool, I then cut different sized donut-shaped rings from the three circles. Their inside diameters were cut to roughly match three different outside diameters of the cone-shaped form, and the cuts were done at an angle to closely conform to the slope of the staves. I did a dry-fit of the jig surrounding the cone shape and positioned pieces of all-thread with nuts and washers at each layer. After removing the jig I applied smooth, slippery duct tape to the inside edges of the donut rings, to reduce fiction against the staves and to allow easier removal later. Then I laid the staves back out with their open inside seams facing up and visually checked once again for any sawdust that might interfere. Because I knew that the tightening all the nuts would take some time, I waited until the next morning when the temperature was cooler, to have a little more working time with the glue.

To assemble the cone I applied glue (Titebond) generously to all the glue surfaces, positioned the staved cone on the mounted faceplate, installed the three donuts with the all-thread, and quickly threaded wing nuts onto the all-thread on the back side of the face plate. By tightening the nuts that I had positioned at each donut, I was able to squeeze the donuts towards the faceplate. **Photo 10-10** shows the glued assembly positioned upside-down to allow glue squeeze-out to drain from the inside. The staves must fit perfectly for this technique to succeed. Building the jig is time consuming, but it does a great job of applying pressure in the needed directions and it results in a perfectly round form, attached and centered on a mounted faceplate, ready for turning.

For demonstration purposes I glued up another of my three cones using another method. Similar to gluing flat segments, I glued together pairs of staves until two halves existed. **Photo 10-11** shows quick clamps applying pressure between two staves with a spline in between. Because of the angles and the widths of the staves, the two outside edges lined up opposite each other and allowed for this type of clamping. If that had not been the case, I would have used numerous rubber bands.

In **photo 10-12**, because the outside profile of the form was not very acute, I was able to use rubber bands to clamp the quarter-sections together. The bands stayed in place without slipping, allowing me to apply many around the shape. This is tricky, the bands must be stretched towards the inside of the form in order to provide uniform pressure on both sides of the glue line, otherwise the rubber-band pressure will try to pull open the outside of the seam. Play around with this dry before gluing and you will see how to adjust the tension.

Now that there are two halves, it is just a matter of truing up the mating surfaces to achieve a perfect fit between the two halves. My 20-inch disc sander makes short work of this chore (**photo 10-13**). Sandpaper mounted on a flat surface is another option, it just takes a little more muscle. A little rough-sanding with a belt sander can reduce the amount of hand-sanding. Once you achieve a perfect fit between the two halves, then it is a simple matter of gluing and clamping them together with rubber bands.

The first two forms, after removing the donut-style clamping device, were center-mounted and ready for turning. I glued the third form to a faceplate-mounted waste block. Next I flattened the base of all three turnings to prepare them for a couple layers of veneer. This presented a compromise in grain orientation: the grain of the staves is vertical, while the grain of the veneer is horizontal. Normally I would not consider such an arrangement, however in this case, because the overall dimensions were quite small, the risks were acceptable. To glue on the two layers of veneer, I used my ceiling clamp system as shown in **photo 10-14** (next page). I glued both layers of veneer at the same time, with just a slight offset of their respective grain directions. To

10-11   This is another method of joining staves.

10-12   Rubber bands can provide plenty of clamping pressure.

10-13   A disc sander makes short work of flattening the half-cones.

10-14   Veneer layers are added, with the clamps pressed against the ceiling..

10-15   A mortise and tenon joint creates a more reliable glue joint.

ensure consistent clamping pressure, the veneers were positioned on a thin, wax-paper covered rubber router pad.

For the base rings, I assembled rings of ebony from segments with their grain oriented vertically, same as the staves. Instead of cutting these miters on the miter saw, I rip-cut strips on the table saw at 22.5° each side, and then used the miter saw (at 90°) to cut these strips into segments. I attached the resulting rings to a waste block with hot-melt, and prepared them for joining to the vessel base. Because of their small size I could have built these base rings of ebony with horizontal grain, but I wanted vertical grain in an upper ring, so it was easier to build both rings the same way. By having vertical grain I was able to create a stronger joint, as described next.

Mortise-and-Tenon Joint Between Layers

I wanted to improve the strength of the joint, so instead of gluing two flat surfaces to each other (the ebony end-grain and the maple veneer side-grain), I decided to join them using a half mortise-and-tenon type of joint. This provided a small side-grain-to-side-grain connection within the seam. **Photo 10-15** shows the vessel base with its half-mortise cut, and the ebony

base ring with its tenon cut. The easiest sequence that I have found for accurately turning this type of connection is:

1. Determine the center of the wall thickness by turning at least one of the profiles (inside or outside) close to its final shape.

2. Use a sharp diamond-pointed scraper to carefully turn a mortise in the base of the vessel, as shown in **photo 10-15.** Turn this mortise diameter close to the intended centerline of the vessel wall thickness. In **photo 10-15**, I have intentionally left more wood to the outside of the vessel until the assembly is complete, when it will be turned down to the final profile.

3. Next, turn the tenon or male portion of the connection as shown in **photo 10-15**. Because of the darkness of the ebony, you must look closely. Temporarily attach the ring of ebony to a circle of MDF and then screw it onto a screw chuck or grab it in a four-jaw chuck. Using calipers that were set to the outside measurement of the mortise, turn the tenon diameter to a very close match, but not all the way. Also, make sure the tenon is slightly longer than the depth of the mortise.

4. Remove the ebony tenon piece from the screw chuck and re-mount the vessel onto

10-16 A tapered plug completes the vessel base.

10-17 In lieu of a steady rest, braces can provide stability.

the lathe. Check the fit, it should still be a little too tight. Using the pointed scraper, remove a smidgen of material from the side of the mortise and check the fit again. Continue removing tiny shavings and checking the fit until it's snug.

5. Check the horizontal gap between the two pieces. It should be slightly open because the tenon has bottomed out in the mortise. Remove tiny amounts from the bottom of the mortise and check frequently until the gap becomes tight.

6. There is no way that I know of for measuring the accuracy of the right-angle side cuts that you need to make. They are so small you should be able to eyeball the surfaces and achieve a good fit.

7. One way to check for tight spots is to insert the tenon into the mortise while the lathe is turning, but burnishing the wood will seal wood pores, which will jeopardize the gluing. I suggest minimizing this type of fit check.

It takes a little time to fit up this type of connection, but the improvement in joint stability is well worth the effort. Even though the side-grain-to-side-grain portion of the joint is quite small, it adds a lot of strength.

Back to Vessel Construction

The next step was to insert a plug into the ebony base ring. I used a piece of curly maple, as shown in **photo 10-16**. When fitting up this kind of plug, remember to shape the plug first, and then cut the recess in the base. It is a lot easier than the other way around.

I turned the outside profiles pretty close to their final shape and sawed the forms off their faceplates, then re-mounted them with their bases glued to the same waste blocks. I turned a shallow recess (about 1/16 inch) into the removed faceplates and used these precisely dimensioned recesses to fit the base ebony rings, thereby keeping everything nicely centered. I did not turn the base ebony rings down to their final diameter, in order to provide more stability and strength for attaching to the waste blocks. Because the base diameters were small, possibly not providing enough strength during the interior turning, I decided to install braces on the outside of the vessels (**photo 10-17**). I did not want to risk losing a piece off its waste block. A steady rest could have been used instead of the braces. The insides were then turn down to a wall thickness of just over 1/8 inch. I figured that later, after shear-scraping and sanding the outside, the final wall thicknesses would be pretty close to 1/8 inch. I

10-18   Veneer layers are added to the vessel top.

10-19   The upper section of the vessel gets prepared.

10-20   The tailstock effectively clamps these sections together.

sanded the inside and then cut a half-mortise into the top, to accommodate the gluing of another ebony ring.

For the second ebony ring I glued together a 3/4-inch tall ring with vertical grain, mounted it on a piece of MDF, and machined it to fit the mortise that you can see at the top of the staves in **photo 10-17**. After gluing the ebony ring onto the staves I parted it off, leaving enough ebony still attached to the MDF to provide another ebony ring for one of the other vessels. I shaped these ebony rings with a mortise, just as I had shaped the top of the staves, in order to accept the next component. The third vessel was a little different: I used East Indian rosewood for the center of the splines and also for the center and top rings, instead of ebony.

I then started constructing the upper portion of the vessel. For the top rims, I created small ebony rings with horizontal grain and mounted them to center-drilled discs of MDF. After I flattened the ebony I glued on two layers of veneer, and cleaned them up as shown in **photo 10-18**.

I had a few nice pieces of maple burl that I had decided to use for the shoulder area of two of the vessels. For the vessel with the rosewood, I used a piece of vertical-grained spalted maple. These burl pieces, with their grain oriented in many directions, were center-drilled and mounted onto a screw chuck (**photo 10-19**). I turned a rough outside shape and created a flat surface in order to glue on the top ebony ring, the one with the veneers.

I unscrewed the shoulder piece (the burl) from the screw chuck and screwed the top ebony ring back onto the chuck. This allowed me to position the tailstock to act as a clamp and centering device for gluing on the burl piece, as shown in **photo 10-20**.

I rough-shaped the inside of the burl piece and cut a half-tenon to fit the top of the ebony ring that was attached to the top of the staves. After achieving a snug fit, I put the two pieces together without glue. This assembly was lathe mounted and I used the tailstock to hold the top onto the lower half. I removed the braces and final-shaped the outside. After taking the assembly apart, I reinstalled the top onto the screw chuck, turned the inside to the finished wall thickness, power-sanded, and then protected it from glue squeeze-out by applying tape (**photo 10-21**). Note the tenon on the burl rim, which will fit the ebony ring.

I glued the two halves together in an upside-down position to prevent glue from running down the inside of the staves. The next day, I turned off the top MDF disc and shear-scraped and sanded the outside. After removing the interior tape I cleaned up the inside seam, wiped the vessel clean with a tack cloth, and applied sanding sealer. If you look closely at the waste block in **photo 10-22**, you'll see that I had to remove part of it in order to accomplish the final turning and sanding near the base. With hindsight, I could have saved myself some trouble by laminating another layer onto the waste block before gluing on the vessel, thus allowing much easier access to the lower section.

After another coat of sanding sealer and four more coats of satin finishing oil, I took the vessels off the waste blocks, reverse-mounted them, and prepared the bases for signature and finishing. The finished vessels are shown in **photo 10-01** (page 88).

One other stave-gluing method that I did not show during the construction of these three vessels is the use of gluing blocks on the outside surfaces of the staves. The donut compression-ring technique does not work very well if the vessel slope is flatter than about 60° and as the slope approaches 45°, it does not work at all. The ratio of vertical pressure compared to horizontal pressure creates an ineffective clamp. My solution to clamping a flatter cone shape all at one time is to temporarily attach glue blocks and use hose clamps. **Photo 10-23** shows this type of arrangement. The glue blocks prevent the hose clamps from sliding on the angled surface.

10-21   Tape can be used to prevent glue squeeze-out contamination.

10-22   Generally, I like to apply finish while the vessel is still mounted.

10-23   Glue blocks can also be used to assemble staves.

11-00   *MADHATTER'S TEACUP* (6-1/2 inches tall) — an example of alternating stave orientation.

11.

Lamination Trickery

Mother Nature does a fine job of creating layers of color in the woods that she grows and solid-wood woodturners experience the joy of exposing those layers to the world. Different shapes and profile angles expose different wood and create a wide array of images. Laminated wood is the same, completely different images appear depending upon the angle of exposure. In this chapter, I offer a few of the many design effects that are possible with layers of wood.

Building Zigzag Rings

Zigzag patterns require precise fitting and gluing. You can use them as a stand-alone feature rings, or as a complementary ring alongside a feature ring, almost any size or shape is possible. The first step is to decide how many zigs and how many zags you want in your ring, that is, how many points upward and downward. To calculate this you need to know the circumference of the ring and the characteristics of the adjoining rings, that is, how many segments or feature ring elements. Let's assume a diameter of 6 inches, therefore, a circumference of 18.85 inches. In addition, assume that the rings next to the zigzag ring contain 12 segments, which means the segments next to the zigzag ring are approximately 1.57 inches long (18.85 inches divided by 12). With this information, you can decide the shape of the zigzag pattern. It can be a flat design with only six upward points (one for every two segments), or it can be a sharper pointed design with 24 upward points (two per segment). For every upward point, there'll be two slopes downward. This means that to create 12 upward points, 24 angled components are required. To create a circumference of 18.85 inches, each of the half-point components needs

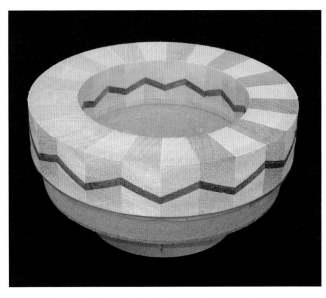

11-01   This is a typical zig-zag feature ring.

to be .79 inch wide (18.85 inches divided by 24 pieces). Another decision relates to the number of layers to laminate in the zigzag, it is just a matter of preparing and gluing together strips. The technique for building the zigzag remains the same regardless of the number of layers. To keep this demonstration reasonably simple, I will build a zigzag ring with just one centered contrasting band of wood. **Photo 11-01** shows a completed 6-inch diameter ring with 12 upward and 12 downward points. Follow along and I will show you how I built this ring

I needed 24 angled pieces of wood .79 inch long; to create a 6-inch diameter ring, I decided to increase the length to .84 inch (a little fudge factor). I laminated three 30-inch strips of wood together: two 5/8-inch wide strips of yellowheart and one 1/8-inch wide strip of purpleheart. The width of the outside strips is important. If they are too narrow, there will not be enough thickness to create the required shape. To illustrate this, I glued together two zigzag components shown in **photo 11-02** (next page). The outlined area of each segment represents the tallest dimension possible from it. As you can see, if I were to transform the assembly on the right into a rectangular segment, there would be no border around the zigzag, and the points of the zigzag might actually become cut off. I constructed the segment on the left with a wider outside strip

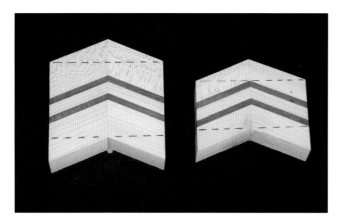

11-02   Be sure that the outside strips of wood are wide enough.

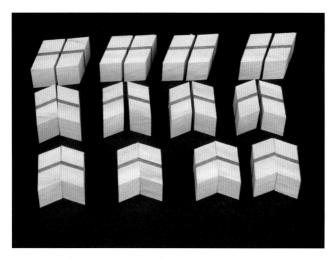

11-03   These were cut from a three-layer lamination.

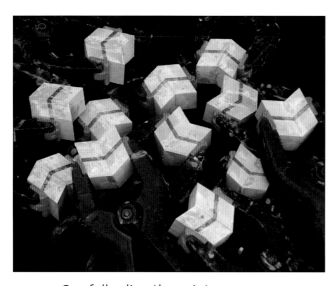

11-04   Carefully align the points.

of wood, thus providing plenty of optional material. Keep this in mind as you design any zigzag configuration.

I cleaned-up my three-strip lamination to prepare it for the miter saw, set the saw at 22.5°, and made a cut at one end. I examined the lamination and confirmed that the center strip of wood was parallel to the outside surfaces. The zigzag pattern will be very difficult to construct accurately if the center strip is out of square. The choice of 22.5° was simply my decision, I could have chosen 15°, 45°, or most any other angle just as easily. This angle determines the sharpness of the zigzag points. Sharper angles produce taller patterns, flatter angles produce shorter patterns.

I set a stop block in order to make a series of angled cuts that measured .84 inch wide. Unlike ring segments, I did not flip the board over during cutting so the cuts are all parallel to each other. I maintained the order in which I cut these angled segments in order to preserve any existing color match when I later reassembled the pieces. A few samples of these angled cuts are positioned at the top of **photo 11-03**.

After cutting 26 pieces (I wanted an extra pair), I flipped over every other one and paired them together (**photo 11-03**).

I lightly disc-sanded the opposing surfaces to ensure nice tight glue joints and then glued them together in pairs. Aligning the purpleheart points on both sides of the joint required extreme care, and a magnifying light was especially helpful. Spring clamps were used, as shown in **photo 11-04**.

Next, I used the disc sander to clean up the glue squeeze-out on both sides of the seam, and trimmed these pairs on the table saw to form rectangular segments.

I ripped a narrow strip of 3/4-inch MDF and stuck a piece of double-sided tape down its length. Holding the MDF strip against the side of my table saw fence and using the fence as a guide, I placed the pieces onto the tape as shown in **photo 11-05**. To position the pieces in a nice straight line, I held the two points

11-05 Double-sided tape can be used to secure segments for table saw trimming.

11-06 The table saw makes short work of creating rectangular segments.

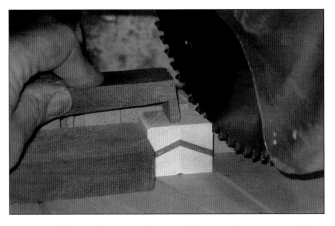

11-07 The miter saw is used to create segments from the rectangular assemblies.

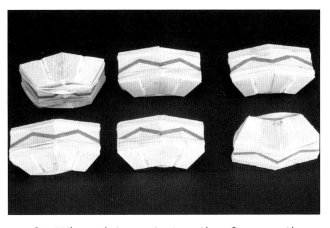

11-08 When gluing pairs together, focus on the point-to-point alignments.

against the fence as I lowered them onto the tape. My left thumb, hidden from view, is pressing the MDF strip against the saw fence. A few good whacks with a rubber mallet ensured a good bond.

Using the table saw, I trimmed the points off the segments (**photo 11-06**) and then adjusted the fence to trim the other side, thus creating rectangles.

Now it is a matter of miter-cutting these segments to form a 12-segment ring (360° divided by 24 angles, equals 15° per end). I adjusted the miter saw angle and locked the stop block to cut one end of each segment. This first cut hardly shortened the overall length of the segments (**photo 11-07**). Then I barely

tapped the stop block a smidgen towards the blade and cut the other ends. If you look at the bottom of the segment, you will see that I left a little bit of the angle indentation. This provided an instant orientation reminder during cutting and assembly. If one segment were to be placed upside-down it would stick out like a sore thumb.

Using a sanding jig, I perfected the 15° angles and dry-fit the ring. Once satisfied that the angles were right on, I glued together six pairs of these segments as shown in **photo 11-08**. If I had glued the ring together all at once or had used the half-ring method, I would have not been able to focus individually on each joint. During all of the gluing steps, the only focus is to align the zigzag points. The top and bottom

11-09   The use of a parting tool creates a two-for-one opportunity.

surfaces can always be trued up later. Don't imagine that the inside alignment is not as important. A perfect outside alignment can easily be turned away, exposing less than perfect alignment within the vessel wall, if the inside is not just as accurately aligned.

I continued the process of joining these segments together until I had two halves. While joining segments, I used the disc sander to expose their mating corners and inspected the intersections before proceeding. I did not want to discover a defective joint later. The half-sections were touched up on the disc sander and then joined together.

The key to successfully aligning all the zigzag points is accurate cutting, sanding, and eye-balling. A few minor errors here and there can accumulate and cause an obvious misalignment within the ring. If the diameter is small and the zigzags are few, then you may need to construct your ring a little differently: instead of joining the first pairs as described, mitering them will create a ring with more corners, thus conforming more closely to the roundness of your vessel. Usually this is not necessary, but it is an option.

You might have noticed while looking at the previous photos that the constructed zigzag ring was quite thick from outside to inside. Normally, this would not be the case. I did it this way to demonstrate another little-used technique, splitting rings concentrically as opposed to horizontally. **Photo 11-09** shows the original zigzag ring parted into two rings: a

11-10   *CHILD'S PLAY* (7 inches diameter) — an example of multi-generational lamination.

freebie so to speak. This is not often useful, but I show it to demonstrate — always be on the lookout for time-saving techniques. With a wider ring, several separate zigzag rings are possible and the initial assembly time would not be any longer.

Multi-Generational Lamination

Now the real fun begins. Instead of building a simple zigzag pattern of consistently up and down points, this technique can produce incredibly complex patterns. You glue laminations together, cut them apart, glue them back together again, and so forth. With each cutting and gluing step, the design becomes more complex. The different angles selected for cutting the lamination apart create different patterns. The number of generations is limited only by your imagination and by your ability to maintain accuracy. Clarence Rannefeld's book, *Laminated Designs in Wood*, explores this subject in great depth. My goal here is to familiarize you with the technique, so you can explore the endless possibilities.

Photo 11-10 shows an example of multi-generational lamination. This design is similar to a zigzag, though more complex. This

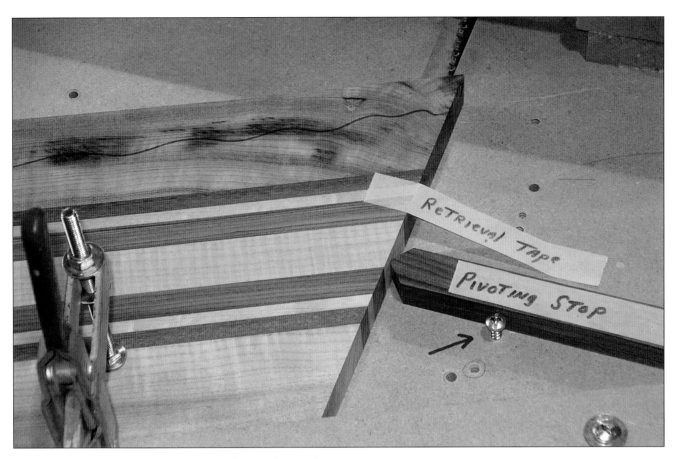

11-11   It starts with cutting strips from a linear lamination.

particular close-up photo is of the top portion of a sculptural piece, *CHILD'S PLAY A.K.A. HARRY POTTER'S TOY* (photo 11-10). The zigzag ring near the top of the sphere was made from the same lamination as the previously described zigzag ring. The design below is more complex, you can count eleven layers of wood mitered into different angles. Laminating eleven layers is the easy part, creating the multiple angles is the challenge. Designing a ring such as shown in **photo 11-10** is very time-consuming; most of the time I wing it without a plan and decide each step as I go, not worrying too much about the exact finished diameter or the exact shape of the zigzags. If you wish to predetermine the outcome, then draw each step on paper and scissor-cut the paper to mimic the table saw. Then reassemble the paper strips to display the results of the next step. If you are a computer whiz, you can draw designs that way. For me, it is more fun to create the design as I cut and glue in the shop. Here's how I build a ring with multiple generations of lamination.

First a linear lamination is needed. I chose five types of wood to create a nine-piece lamination about 32 inches long. The four strips on either side of the center strip were milled and arranged to create mirror images. Because of the multiple steps involved, a lot of wood is reduced to sawdust. Normally, a 32-inch long strip of wood would produce enough segments to create a 10-inch diameter ring. In this case, the largest diameter will be drastically smaller because each step (or generation) reduces the length of the lamination. Every strip of wood in the lamination must be perfectly dimensioned before gluing. This technique makes cumulative errors a big concern. Each step depends upon the accuracy of the previous steps. A drum sander is particularly valuable for dimensioning.

After cleaning up the lamination, I prepared a table saw sled for angled crosscutting. I modified the same sled that I used to cut the compound miters in Chapter 10. The sled's

11-12   A drum sander can ensure consistent thicknesses and smooth surfaces.

11-13   A gluing jig can help keep components square during gluing.

previous wide kerf was closed by gluing in an angled piece of MDF, and I adjusted the miter fence to about 25° (the exact angle is not critical for this step). **Photo 11-11** shows the lamination clamped in place and ready for cutting. Notice the width of the outside strips of myrtlewood. Just as with simple zigzag segments, much of the outside strip can become waste.

I installed a pointed, pivoting stop to cut 1/2-inch wide strips. To use this type of stop, secure one end with a screw and install another screw to act as a stop for the stop block. A red arrow in the photo points to the stop screw. With the pivoting stop held against the screw and the lamination end held against the stop block and fence, lock the hold-down clamp into position. Pivoting the stop out of the way makes it possible to retrieve the cutoff as soon as it is free; otherwise, it becomes confined between the blade and an immovable stop block. With my left hand pushing the sled, I can grasp a piece of applied masking tape (as shown) with my right hand and safely retrieve the cutoff. It is always a good idea to avoid loose pieces of wood near a moving saw blade. If this method of cutting makes you nervous, then a hold-down clamp on the cutoff side is an option. The disadvantage of a hold-down clamp, in addition to the extra step, is that it requires bringing the cut-off back alongside the moving blade, which can leave unwanted scoring marks on the wood.

The table saw with a freshly sharpened crosscut blade does a great job of producing ultra-smooth cuts. Because the wood grain direction is at an angle to the blade, a crosscut blade is more effective than a rip blade. There is a temptation to glue the pieces together directly from the saw, however, I know that a better glue joint is possible by sanding the surfaces. In this case, because of the length of the strips, a disc sander will not work. For a tray for making several light passes through a drum sander I used a piece of 3/4-inch MDF, covered with 80-grit sandpaper to avoid slippage. **Photo 11-12** shows the tray packed with the cutoffs. Before sanding the pieces, I used the miter saw to square the ends, because I did not want an angled, unsupported end to go through the drum sander. I arranged the pieces end-to-end, with the wood grain facing into the rotation of the drum. To prevent the spinning drum from throwing one of the cutoffs, I attached a small rail of wood to the end of the tray and positioned the cutoffs against this rail. I took great care to ensure that the pieces rested flat on the tray. Small debris can prevent a piece from lying flat, causing an uneven surface. After sanding one side, I flipped the pieces and lightly sanded the other sides.

It's a challenge to accurately glue all these pieces back together into a flat zigzag design. Accomplishing the glue job in one step is desirable but not practical. Therefore, I

11-14   Maintaining accurate point to point alignment is critical.

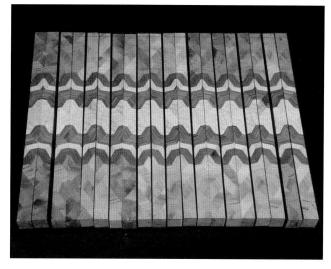

11-15   A new pattern emerges as a result of another series of cuts.

assembled eight pieces at a time as shown in **photo 11-13**. I used a wax paper-covered MDF gluing tray with a 90° stop (the blue-taped piece at the left end). First, I dry-fit the pieces to ensure that all the points lined up when all the ends were positioned against the stop. It was important to align the points and to be sure that the eight pieces were glued square.

I passed the glued sections of eight through the drum sander to remove the glue squeeze-out, and proceeded to join them into one continuous lamination. A few very light disc sander touch-ups created tight glue lines between the sections of eight. **Photo 11-14** shows this stage of the project. I once more passed the completed lamination through the drum sander, then the edges were squared up on the table saw: the two long edges must be parallel with the zigzags as well as with each other. When gluing together an arrangement such as this, it is important that not only do the points line up, but also that the elements form a straight line from end to end.

Where to make the next cut? To create a uniform, mirror-image design, the next set of cuts must all pass through identical locations on opposite sides of the center strip. The astuteness of the next cut will determine the appearance of the next generation. By drawing a few pencil lines directly on the lamination and imagining every other piece flipped over, it

is possible to visualize the next design shape. The sharper the angle, the more dramatic the results. Play around with the options to decide your next move.

I selected two glue lines on opposite sides of the lamination, about 3 inches offset from each other, as my alignment for the next set of cuts. Here is where things start to get interesting. The cuts must create perfect mirror images on either side of the blade. Otherwise, when the pieces are flipped over and re-glued, the alignment will not be correct. To do this, I positioned the lamination on the sled with the two seams that I had selected directly centered on the sled kerf, and I relocated the miter fence with the hold-down clamp against the lamination. The sharpness of the angle prompted me to attach a strip of 80-grit sandpaper to the fence to help eliminate slippage. For this operation a stop block was not used, each cut was individually eyeballed over the kerf. Achieving perfect mirror images on either side of the blade is just about impossible by eyeballing, but I will be able to correct minor differences later. For this step, my goal was to achieve the closest mirror images that I could.

Look at **photo 11-14** and visualize the lamination cut into angled 3/4-inch wide strips; **photo 11-15** shows those new strips. To create matching pairs I have turned over every other strip and squared all the ends. An entirely different

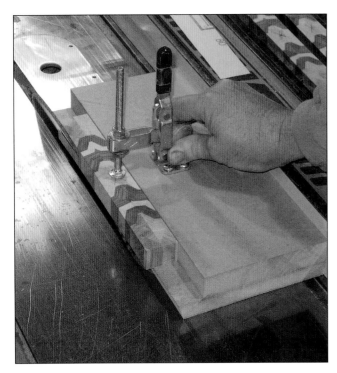

11-16   A simple sled enables safe and accurate trimming of small strips.

11-17   Accuracy of both the saw cuts and the point to point alignments is critical.

pattern has emerged. The process of cutting and reassembling can continue, though the limitations of standard woodworking equipment and my difficulty maintaining accuracy usually make it impractical to continue beyond one more generation. I decided to stop this particular project at this stage.

The next step was to glue together the pairs shown in **photo 11-15**. I used the drum sander with the same tray to sand their mating surfaces. Because of minor misalignments (from eyeballing the table saw cuts), I passed the surfaces through the sander multiple times. Before each pass I examined the mirror images and positioned whichever side needed more trimming. Using spring clamps, I glued the pairs to form ten pieces.

The next challenge was to transform these ten pieces into segmented staves that would form a ring — a tricky task because so many elements must line up while being joined with tight mitered seams. I cleaned them up, examined them, and selected the best surfaces for the outside of the ring. The accuracy of the intersections up to this stage was acceptable,

even though a few tiny mismatches existed. After examining the next set of dry glue joints, I decided to improve the alignments by making a series of very tiny rip cuts on the sides of the pieces. My goal was to create identical edges that would align perfectly with each other. With the saw fence adjusted to remove just a smidgen, I examined each piece and selected whichever side needed trimming. After making ten trim cuts, I tapped the fence towards the blade and repeated the process. I did this about three times, trimming whichever edge seemed longer, until all the opposing edges would align.

Because of the length of the pieces, I cut the miters on the table saw instead of the miter saw. These tall, narrow pieces needed an 18° miter on each side. I did not like the prospect of pushing them through the saw blade with just the saw fence as a guide, because after cutting their two sides the narrow bottom side would be unstable on the table. In addition, I wanted ultra-smooth cuts that would require little or no sanding.

A simple sled was the answer. I used two rectangular pieces of MDF: a piece 1 inch thick glued onto a slightly wider piece of 3/4 inch. The

11-18   Successful gluing requires practice and planning.

ten laminated pieces were slightly thinner than 1 inch, therefore the 1-inch MDF provided an effective stop block on the sled. This sled (shown in **photo 11-16**) simply provided a means of smoothly transporting the segments (staves) through the blade, achieving a much smoother cut than would be possible using the table fence alone. Before making the final cuts, I rip-cut a test strip of 1-inch MDF 2 inches wide, 18° on each side. I made crosscuts from this strip and assembled a test ring to check the accuracy of the blade setting.

To eliminate unwanted stave movement, I used a toggle-style hold down clamp to secure the pieces to the sled. The clamp also provided a nice handle. I cut one side of all the pieces, tapped the fence towards the blade just a smidgen, and cut the other sides. The sled, along with a sharp 80-tooth crosscut blade, did a remarkable job of producing acceptable ready-to-glue surfaces.

A dry-fit of the ten pieces confirmed the angles were right on, but what about the alignment of all the intersections? Before dry-fitting the pieces, I arranged them side by side to achieve

the best fit. I secured them with rubber bands (**photo 11-17**) and adjusted the ends to align everything as closely as possible. With the cylinder of staves still secured, I sanded both ends on the disc sander. I did this twice with tiny adjustments each time, striving for the best alignments. The alignment match between pieces was not perfect, but they were all very close. The cylinder end-sanding allowed all-at-one-time gluing without the need to inspect point intersections. With the cylinder vertical (as in **photo 11-17**), a few taps with a hammer would reposition everything as it had been during the dry-fit. Before disassembling the dry-fit, I also wrapped a few pieces of masking tape around the assembly and cut the tape on one seam, to further ensure that the pieces would go back together as desired.

I glued the assembly at one time. If I had glued pairs together, there would have been a risk that the final joint points would not align. By gluing it at one time, perhaps tiny misalignments would exist, but I knew that I would not experience a major mismatch within a seam.

I wanted plenty of working time so I decided upon Titebond Extend. If the temperature had been warmer I probably would have used Gorilla Glue or possibly plastic resin glue. The pieces received a last dusting with canned air, the hose clamps were adjusted and ready, a drill with a socket bit for the hose clamps was nearby, a hammer and a thin piece of scrap wood for spreading the glue was awaiting. **Photo 11-18** shows the assembly laid out flat and ready for glue. The masking tape holding the staves together in alignment made the clamping very easy. Pre-glue prep is always smart; wasting glue working time while looking for tools can lead to problems.

I later incorporated the created cylinder into a vessel titled *SCRAMBLED MITERS*, as displayed in **photo 11-19** (next page). In the world of multi-generation laminations, this was a relatively simple project. Designs that are much more complex are possible by continuing the process of cutting and reassembling. Extremely precise

11-19   *SCRAMBLED MITERS* (10 inches tall) — it's not as difficult as it appears.

milling and accurate gluing are essential to success. A tiny compromise early in the project easily produces more noticeable errors later. This type of segmented woodturning is very time-consuming and risky, things can easily go wrong. For the experienced woodworker looking for a challenge, this could be just the answer, good luck!

Two Ways to Build Diamonds

Diamonds are a girl's best friend, and the shape is also attractive on the side of a woodturning. They are much simpler to create compared to multi-generation laminations. One method of creating diamond shapes involves extensive disc sanding, while the other method relies on a router. The disc sander technique is a variation of the feature ring building technique described in Chapter 7: you surround a diamond-shaped piece of wood with other pieces of wood and use the disc sander to create straight and smooth gluing surfaces between the components. **Photo 11-20** shows a typical diamond segment, a leftover from a large ring of diamonds.

In the photo I have labeled the four sides and marked with a pen all the glue lines that required disc sanding. To build this diamond:

Using the miter saw I cut the center diamond shape. For appearances, I wanted the grain direction of the curly maple to match the grain direction outside the diamond; notice that all the curly maple grain is vertical.

Two sides of the diamond (#1 and #4) were lightly disc-sanded, then I glued on thin pieces of purpleheart to both sides at the same time. The purpleheart pieces and all the other to-be-added pieces were cut slightly longer than needed, which simplified the gluing steps.

I carefully sanded sides #2 and #3, and sanded the ends of the previously glued-on purpleheart pieces flush with the side of the diamond.

I glued on two more strips of purpleheart to sides #2 and #3. This process of sanding and gluing two sides at a time continued until all the components were in place. If you study the lines in the photo you'll be able to visualize the order of assembly.

With the diamond shape surrounded, it was then only a matter of squaring the rectangle and mitering two edges to create a segment for ring construction.

The easiest way to make a mistake is to sand too aggressively, thereby removing too much width from the previous layer. I mentioned that the diamond shown in **photo 11-20** was a reject. Look closely: the thin strip of maple on side #2 is thinner than the other similar strips, a result of too much sanding. A very minor defect, but because I had made a couple of extras, I had better choices. A slight variation of this technique, which does a better job of hiding the last outside glue lines, is described in Chapter 15.

The second technique is trickier. **Photo 11-21** shows a very elongated diamond shape on the lower portion of a vessel. These diamonds are actually small 1/2-inch squares positioned on edge at a 45° angle. The elongated shape resulted from shaping the vessel wall at an acute angle. So, how did I do this using a router?

First, I built the diamonds by sandwiching a 3/8-inch thick board of holly between two thin layers of ebony.

I then cut small strips from the lamination, passed the strips through a drum sander, and glued two more thin layers of ebony to the other sides of the holly strips as seen in **photo 11-22**. The goal was to create 1/2-inch square strips. I band-sawed the glued assembly into individual strips, which I cleaned up and squared with a little handwork and the drum sander. I then cut them into about 2-1/2 inch lengths.

I used a very simple jig, shown in **photo 11-23** (next page), to cut V notches into the ends of segments. The jig is nothing more than a straight edge clamped to a smooth surface. A bar clamp holds a segment in place so that a router bit can cut the notch. The bit has to be a 90° V shape. It requires a little fiddling to get everything centered and at the right depth; multiple passes with a stop on a plunge-router works best. The goal is to create two opposing notches that will fit around the square piece of holly/ebony. I try to cut the notches just a tiny bit too deep, then I disc-sand to remove tiny increments from the segment ends until a perfect snug fit exists. When lightly sanding the segment ends, address both ends of the notch. The fit around the diamond piece has to be snug

11-20   A disc sander can create straight, tight glue joints.

11-21   An example of router-created diamond-shaped elements.

11-22   To create a diamond with a border, surround it with a contrasting wood.

11-23   Firmly clamp the segment before cutting the notch.

11-24   After installing the diamond, you can treat the segment like any other.

from end to end, with no gap between the pointed segment ends.

Photo 11-24 shows a couple of the diamonds that I made for the vessel shown in **photo 11-21.** Essentially, I have embedded a diamond within a segment. The elongated diamond shape on the vessel wall is simply the result of an angled cut through the segment.

In this diamond assembly the holly and ebony components were oriented with their end-grain perpendicular to the outside of the vessel. I did this intentionally. If I had oriented the wood grain parallel to the vessel wall, the turning would have exposed fragile short grain at the upper point of the diamond, which would easily break away and leave a defective surface. With the end grain oriented perpendicular, the wood fibers stayed in place. We learn from our mistakes! The grain of diamonds used in a vertical portion of a vessel could instead be oriented to match the other segment components.

Laminated Segments and Staves (Five Examples)

An easy way to produce dramatic designs is to use laminated wood as your raw material. The three turnings displayed are examples of laminated segment/stave trickery. The turning *WATERMELON CACTUS* (**photo 11-25**) was built with segments cut from a laminated board with the layers oriented vertically. The lathe shaping exposed the layers and the pattern of oval shapes emerged. *TEACUP FOR ALICE* (**photo 11-26**) resulted from turning a cylinder of laminated staves that I offset-mounted on the lathe. I built *CURVES* (**photo 11-27**) using laminated segments with the layers at an angle within the segments. No curved pieces of wood were used in any of these constructions.

To demonstrate these techniques I laminated strips of cherry and jarrah (**photo 11-28**) with a layer of maple and walnut veneer in between. I used these laminated boards to cut and glue together five different assemblies.

To achieve any kind of effect, I must expose the layers within the lamination. Sharper outside ring corners, which require deeper cutting to create a round ring, will result in more dramatic

11-25 *WATERMELON CACTUS* (21 inches tall) — an example of vertically oriented segment layers.

11-26 *TEACUP FOR ALICE* (4 inches tall) — an example of off-centered laminated staves.

11-27 *CURVES* (29 inches tall) — an example of angled layers within a laminated segment.

11-28   Laminated strips can be cut many different ways for different effects.

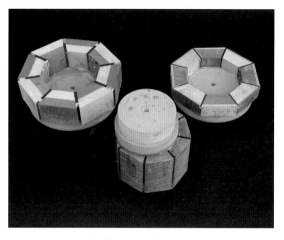

11-29   From left to right, vertical layers, an off-centered staved cylinder, and angled layers.

11-30   The lamination modified to reposition layers.

11-31   Three different results from the same laminated strips.

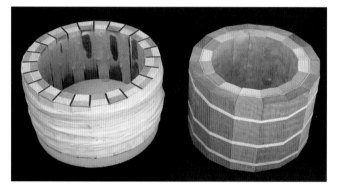

11-32   Two cylinders, constructed differently from the same laminated strips.

designs. **Photo 11-29** shows three different rings made from the laminated material of **photo 11-28** The ring on the left was made from eight segments with the veneer layers vertical within the segments. For the ring on the right, I re-cut the laminated board to orient the veneer at a 45° angle (**photo 11-30**) before I cut the segments. I built the ring in the center by cutting eight staves from the original laminated material, which then was offset-mounted onto a waste block. All three rings came from the same laminated material, but the layers are oriented very differently.

When turned, the three rings display completely different images. **Photo 11-31** shows the transformations. The results are intriguing even though the effort was minor. For the designs to emerge uniformly the rings must be perfectly round, otherwise obvious differences will appear. The cylinder in the center dramatically displays the effect of non-centered laminations.

The next two examples relate to staved construction. **Photo 11-32** shows two cylinders. The one on the left has 24 staves with the position of two woods alternating around the outside (and inside). The trick is to expose the layers by turning a ribbed surface; the actual pattern depends upon the width and depth of the coves. On the left side of **photo 11-39**, I show the same cylinder after a few minutes of turning — a very dramatic effect with very little effort.

The fifth example starts with the cylinder on the right of **photo 11-32**. I have not yet glued the cylinder together, but I have confirmed the fit. My objective was to create a vertically ribbed surface with oval shapes on the ribs. One approach would have been to glue this ring together and then use carving tools to create a ribbed surface. However I am not much of a carver — I prefer to do my carving on the lathe whenever possible. After all, what is a lathe but a carving tool? To shape these individual staves on the lathe, I mounted them two at a time as shown in **photo 11-33**. Using double-sided tape, I attached two staves to a third piece of wood. I do not own a small 4-jaw chuck for my mini-lathe, so instead I used a cup-shaped drive at the headstock end and a live center at the tailstock. If you look closely at the tailstock end of the staves, you'll see that I applied an additional piece of tape across the ends to help keep the staves together. The middle piece of wood does two things: its thickness determines the radius of cut, and the live center can press on it without forcing the two staves apart.

Before miter-cutting the staves, I had to choose their width. I drew a sketch, which allowed me to predict the results of various turning radiuses. **Photo 11-34** shows a layout of rectangles, miter angles, and likely turning profiles. As you can see, the thickness of the spacer wood affects the turning profile. If the spacer is too thick, the radius will be too large (flat) and the oval pattern will not emerge. If the spacer is too narrow, the radius will be too small (sharp) and the turning action will remove the mitered sides, leaving nothing to use as a glue surface.

Photo 11-35 displays the results of turning the pair of staves shown in **photo 11-33**. The layers that form the oval are quite thin, any more turning and they would disappear. At 1 inch wide, these staves are relatively small, there would be more leeway with a larger stave. After turning the staves I smoothed them with a palm sander, using a little piece of double-sided tape to hold the stave in place during sanding.

I then covered the outside stave surfaces with

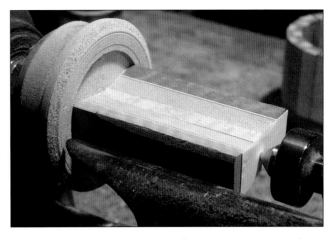

11-33　Staves can be turned two at a time, with a spacer in between.

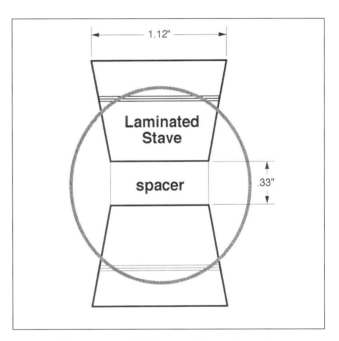

11-34　The spacer thickness determines the shape of the oval and the profile of the stave.

11-35　Carefully turn away the outside layers.

11-37   Before assembling the staves, attach contrasting splines of veneer.

11-38   Before assembling the cylinder, first glue together pairs.

11-39   Completely different results have been obtained from the same type of material.

masking tape and attached walnut veneers to both sides of each stave. **Photo 11-37** shows the gluing of one side. Originally I had planned to use a single layer of veneer between each pair of staves, but the veneer was so thin I doubled the thickness by gluing a piece to both sides. It's tricky to join 16 staves with rounded profiles. To attempt it while also inserting veneer strips would have been foolhardy. To ensure success I not only pre-glued the veneer, but also began by gluing together pairs as shown in **Photo 11-38**.

With the eight pairs of staves positioned in a ring formation, I applied a few rubber bands and wrapped a few revolutions of masking tape around the cylinder. This allowed me to remove the bands, cut the tape down one seam, and lay the staves flat with the open inside seams face up. I applied glue to the seams and rolled the form back together, then aligned all the inside corners to one another and applied many rubber bands.

The protective masking tape on the outside of the staves was a big help, but handwork with a utility knife and a small carving tool was still required to clean up the seams. An 80-grit sanding mop sped the clean-up process. **Photo 11-39** shows this example on the right, along with the previously described example. You might wonder where could such techniques be used? I used this last trick in the construction of a turning titled *FOR GAUDI*, in **photo 11-40**.

Lamination trickery is a fascinating aspect of segmented turning. I have only scratched the surface with these five examples. For years, turners have precisely layered and turned items such as lamps and rolling pins. Virginia Dotson, a well-known turner in Arizona, has achieved great success turning laminated assemblies. Combining some of these techniques could produce results that are even more stunning. Give it some thought and see what innovations you can discover.

11-40 *FOR GAUDI* (18 inches tall) — an example of pre-turned staves.

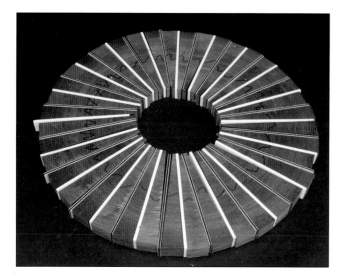

11-42   This project requires 40 segments and 40 splines.

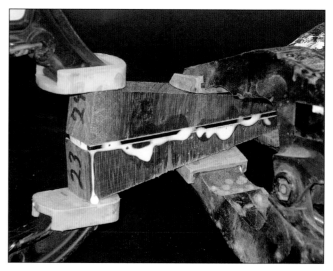

11-43   Assembly starts by gluing pairs together with splines.

A Bowl from a Board

You might be thinking that segmented turning uses a lot less wood compared to conventional turning because there is very little hollowing involved. You would be wrong. In conventional segmented ring construction, many board feet of good wood goes into the trash. Many years ago at an AAW symposium, Mike Shuler, a well-known woodturner from Santa Cruz, California, demonstrated making a bowl with very little waste. He had advanced a technique based on construction methods used in the salad bowl industry. Shuler also credits Dale Nish, in his classic book *Creative Woodturning*, for describing the technique of stacking angled rings band-sawn from boards to create a bowl shape. This is a great example of how sharing ideas leads to innovation and the whole field of woodturning advances one more step. That is not to say that we should all copy each other's ideas, there is a big difference between plagiarism and what Shuler describes as, "spring-boarding from an existing concept." With Mike Shuler's encouragement, I will describe the basics of this ingenious technique. I offer it so you can use the basic technique and possibly take another step in a new direction.

Instead of cutting, gluing, and stacking individual rings, I will glue together two large half-rings and then band-saw angled rings that will be stacked into a bowl shape. I chose a board of straight-grained purpleheart about 5-1/2 inches wide by 30 inches long. Using my miter saw, I cut 40 segments with a 4.5° angle on each side (80 times 4.5° equals 360°). I cut the pointed ends of the segments less than 1/4 inch wide. Before cutting the segments, I laminated pieces of maple veneer and thin ebony together in order to create 20 splines that I will glue between every other segment. For the other 20 seams, I cut the same size spline from solid holly. These unglued segments and splines are shown in **photo 11-42**.

Sanding segments of this size presents a challenge because of the length of the glue lines and the short length of the wood grain. Just a little bit of sanding heat will warp the surface. Actually, just releasing wood tension by cutting such short, wide segments can result in some warping. It is certainly tempting to glue without sanding, but I know I can improve the glue lines, so I sand. First, I changed the paper on my disc sander. Sharp, fresh sandpaper will reduce time on the disc and therefore reduce heat build-up. A dry-fit of the segments confirmed that my cuts were right on and that very little sanding would be necessary. I decided to freehand-sand half of the seams and then glue those 20 pairs together with a laminated spline in between (**photo 11--43**). To minimize warping, I sanded the segments in stages, just a little sanding followed

11-44　Gluing cauls apply pressure in the right direction.

11-45　The two half-sections will not be glued together.

by cooling time while I sanded the next. After a couple of very light sandings, the joints were ready for glue. I performed the bright light check on each seam and waited for any sanding heat to dissipate before gluing each of the 20 pairs. Never attempt to glue warm segments, the glue will set too quickly and you won't have enough alignment time. Perfect glue joints are vital, one bad joint and the whole project is a loss. Unlike other ring-construction where there is an opportunity to replace a bad ring, with this technique replacing a single defective ring is not an option.

I continued to assemble the large ring by joining pairs to form groups of four and then groups of eight, with two groups of four left alone. The sections of eight required a gluing caul to apply perpendicular clamping pressure. I attached triangular pieces of MDF with a bead of hot-melt glue, as shown in **photo 11-44**. With smaller segments rubber bands provide adequate clamping pressure, but with segments this large, I chose small bar clamps. In **photo 11-44,** I am gluing the center seam, the other seams were previously glued. Before each gluing stage I performed a dry-fit and made minor disc sanding adjustments to ensure that the ring stayed round. It is critical that the final ring shape be perfectly

round, not oval. If any minor adjustments are necessary I want to spread them across many seams, I do not want to make a major adjustment near the end of the construction.

Each half-ring now consisted of two sections of eight and one section of four. Another dry-fit followed by a few minor disc sanding adjustments resulted in two matching halves. To glue these (**photo 11-45**), I used the half-ring method as described in Chapter 7. I only had to deal with three sections and two splines per side, which made the job relatively easy. After this step, unlike conventional segment ring building, I did not join the two halves into a solid ring. I smoothed the surfaces using the disc sander and drum sander, placed the last holly splines in between the halves, and dry-clamped them together with a hose clamp.

To create a bowl shape from this large flat ring required cutting angled rings whose top and bottom diameters matched the diameters of adjacent rings. There are choices: how narrow and at what angle should the rings be cut? Narrow cuts will result in more rings and a taller bowl, but if the rings are too narrow the walls may be too thin, resulting in disaster. The size and shape of the angled rings will determine and limit your bowl shape options. Using the

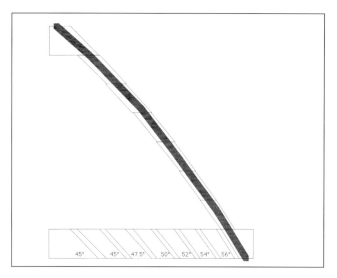

11-46   Carefully plan the location of band-saw cuts.

11-47   Cut carefully: the whole project depends upon following the lines.

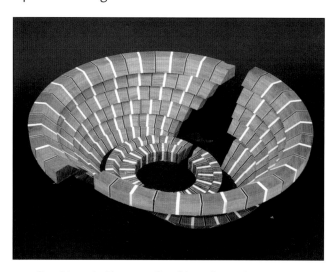

11-48   Here is the result of band-sawing.

actual dimensions of my ring, I have drawn the layout I used for this bowl in **photo 11-46**. To be on the safe side, I allowed almost 1/8 inch for saw-kerf loss. To achieve a slight curve I drew the rings a little wider, with a slightly steeper angle than necessary toward the inside (the bottom of the bowl). This layout resulted in less height because fewer rings could be cut — not a big deal, the bowl is tall enough. If your goal is maximum vessel height with minimum waste, then you must lay out cuts that are steeper and closer together. In any layout, make sure your diameters line up to provide you with adequate wall thickness. It's tempting to cut very thin rings and thus create a taller vessel, but for me the risk is not worth the extra height. In addition, if you cut very thin rings you eliminate room for error and you limit the bowl profile to almost a straight line. Straight lines are not necessarily bad, but I wanted a slight curve.

After deciding on my layout I used a compass to draw concentric circles on the two half-rings that were still clamped together. I separated the two halves and, using a 1/2-inch fine-toothed blade, proceeded to band-saw the cuts. As I made successive cuts, I adjusted the blade angle to achieve the results as drawn. In **photo 11-47**, I am carefully making a cut; a lack of focus here and the whole project is lost. The half-rings are shown in **photo 11-48**.

The remainder of the project was straightforward. I glued the half-rings together with a small piece of holly in between, built ebony and holly rings for the top and bottom, stacked the layers together one at a time, and turned the bowl shape, titled *BLACKBERRY SWIRL*, that you can see in **photo 11-49**.

The technique of using band-sawn angled rings has been around for many years, but as far as I know, with the exception of Mike Shuler, whose turnings are much more complex than this example, few turners have experimented with it or tried to take it to a new level. As I write these words, images of combining other lamination tricks in combination with this technique enter my head. I hope your own brain is spinning with ideas.

11-49   *BLACKBERRY SWIRL* (6-1/2 inches tall) — a very efficient use of lumber.

12-01   *QUILTED BOWLS* (5-1/2 inches tall) — the result of production turning techniques.

12.
Production Turning

One does not normally associate segmented turning with production turning. Most segmented work tends to be one of a kind, built one piece at a time. However, occasionally I do a production run of half a dozen turnings, to meet a Christmas gift deadline or perhaps to quickly re-stock a gallery with lower-priced items.

Such was the case with the six bowls that I profile in this chapter. There are many advantages to constructing multiples of the same design, even though the work can be quite tedious. The design for this production run is a small open bowl shape consisting of 29 layers or rings. In the drawing that follows, I did not bother to number the veneer layers, but they do account for 72 pieces of wood. I made the top four rings and the bottom four rings using 18

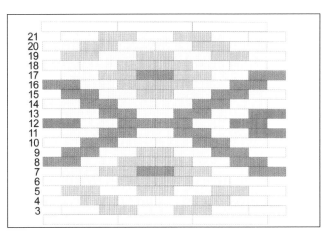

12-03   Without a sketch showing the color arrangement, gluing would be very difficult.

segments each, while the remaining rings consisted of 36 segments each — a total of 901 pieces of wood counting the bottom plug. Considering I made six bowls, that adds up to more than 5,000 small segments. It was a lot of work, but not as much as you might think. **Photo 12-01** displays the six completed bowls.

The first step is to create the design. With a project such as this, I needed two designs: the bowl shape and ring dimensions (**photo 12-02**), and the arrangement of the brick-laid colored segments in each ring design (**photo 12-03**). I

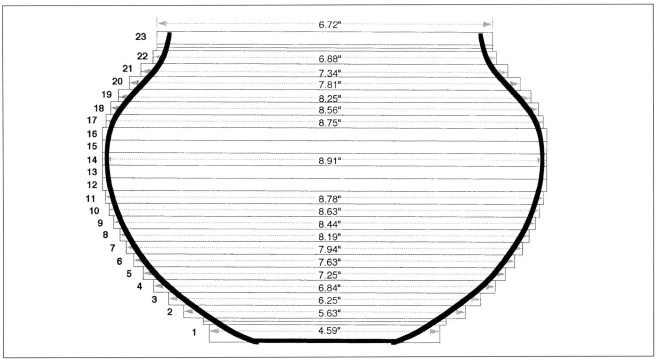

12-02   It all starts with a drawing.

drew the shape design just as any other, though I did not bother to overlay rectangles to determine the segment widths because they were almost all the same. The rings were all built from 5/8-inch wide strips, except for a few wider rings near the top and bottom, which I determined by using my calipers on the drawing. Using the blueprint information I created a cutting list with the segment length information.

I chose 36 segments per ring so I could repeat a pattern six times around the vessel. The actual layout of the colored segments required a little doodling. I used the same layout for all six vessels, but I substituted different woods, creating three different combinations. **Photo 12-03** (previous page) displays the arrangement of segments. To calculate the number of each type of segment per ring, it was a matter of counting the different colored rectangles in the drawing and then multiplying by 6 (the layout drawing is only 1/6 of the circumference). It is very easy to make a mistake while cutting and gluing so many different colored segments. Instead of "measure twice, cut once," it's more like "check three times, glue once." I made a checklist for each of the three different designs that included the number of segments of each type of wood per ring. I also made three different layout drawings to guide assembly. Even with these aids, it is easy to make an arrangement error. You have to stay on your toes.

I constructed the top and bottom portions of the bowls using standard techniques, building the ebony and maple rings from 3/4-inch material and then splitting them into two rings, thus saving a little ring-building time. Constructing all the multicolored rings consumes the most time. Sanding so many individual segment-ends was just too much trouble, so my plan was to cut perfect miters and sand only the light-colored to light-colored joints, which still accounted for a lot of sanding. The design called for rings about 1/4 inch tall. My plan was to construct rings from 3/4-inch material and then split each one into two rings, thereby cutting ring assembling time in half. Each 3/4-inch thick ring would produce two identical 1/4-inch

12-04   Three sets of 3/4-inch tall rings (same pattern, but different woods).

tall rings, therefore 21 colored rings would produce two identical bowls. I milled the boards to a consistent thickness, ripped strips for the widest segments first, and proceeded to glue using Titebond, rubber bands, and the gluing jig shown in Chapter 7 (**photo 7-16**). This required a couple of days of monotonous cutting, sanding, and gluing. I sanded only the ends of the light-colored to light-colored seams, which I rub-joint glued separately, before using the rubber band gluing jig (Chapter 7) to assemble the rings. I used the half-ring method of gluing (Chapter 7). Gang-cutting two segments at a time helped to speed the process and I maintained ring identity by labeling them with a marking pen. **Photo 12-04** shows sixty-three, 3/4-inch tall, colored rings (twenty-one rings of each color combination), the six bases, and three ebony rings, which will become the six top rings.

It was then time to split the colored rings, thereby creating six sets of 21 rings each. The options were to part them on the lathe, or to partially part them followed by band-sawing, or (as I decided) to cut them on the table saw. I flattened both surfaces of the rings on the disc sander and smoothed the outside circumference slightly, so the rings would easily rotate in a cutting jig. At first glance the table-saw technique might appear risky, but I

12-05   Splitting the rings using a table-saw jig creates six different sets.

12-06   Many layers await assembly.

accomplished it without any problems or safety compromises. I used a jig (**photo 12-05**), which I normally use to cut spline slots into picture frame corners. Instead of sliding the jig along the saw fence I clamped it in place, centered and with the blade raised just high enough to cut through the rings. Keeping my hands well above the blade location, I lowered each ring onto the blade and, while maintaining solid ring contact with the side of the jig, rotated it into the blade's rotation. Maintaining a firm grip prevented the blade from grabbing a ring. This operation reduced hours of lathe-parting work to just minutes, while producing smooth surfaces and consistent thicknesses. I would not recommend this method for splitting smaller rings because your fingers would be too close to the saw blade, creating a risky, unsafe situation.

The result, as shown in **photo 12-06,** was six stacks of thin rings, two sets of each color combination. One surface of each ring was already smooth and flat from the previous disc sanding.

To assemble these rings into bowl shapes, I divided each stack of rings into thirds; **photo 12-02** shows the ring numbering. I attached the #8 rings and the #14 rings onto MDF waste blocks using a continuous bead of hot-melt

glue. I also attached the top rings of ebony to waste blocks so that I could add additional colored rings to the upper portion of the bowls. An assortment of these types of MDF waste-block circles is shown in Chapter 7 (**photo 7-24**). I lathe-mounted and flattened the gluing surfaces of these 18 mounted rings using a four-jaw chuck. Next I attached the adjoining 18 rings (# 7, #13, and #20) to another set of waste blocks, centered and attached with six short beads of hot-melt glue. By using MDF circles that are similar in diameter to the rings, centering can be eyeballed. Just a quick touch-up on the disc sander and they were ready for gluing to their mates. I used the carriage bolt/wing nut technique as described in Chapter 7 to glue all these rings together. Each joint consisted of a lathe-flattened surface on one side of the seam and a disc sander-flattened surface on the other side. After each joint cured, I used a utility knife to remove its waste block, scraped the MDF circle clean of hot melt, and if necessary, reduced its diameter to accommodate the next ring. The advantage of the carriage bolt technique is accurate centering. The rotational alignment of each ring is another story. The individual segments were quite small (average .7 inch long), which made it easy to eyeball the segment centers of one ring to the segment

12-08   All six bowls are in various stages of construction.

12-07   This is a section of one bowl being assembled, one layer at a time.

seams of the next ring. However, with so many rings it is difficult to accurately maintain the designed pattern. The trick is to focus not only on the adjoining ring, but also on the first ring in the stack. If you focus only on the adjoining ring, then cumulative errors can produce an obvious distortion in the pattern. **Photo 12-07** shows one of the #8 rings, lathe-mounted with successive rings added. In the photo, the outside

waste block is about to be removed and the smallest ring is about to be prepared for the next ring.

This probably seems like a long process, but it actually went quite quickly. The next photo (**12-08**) shows the progress. In the upper left corner, three of the bowls are starting to take shape: I have glued rings #8 through #3 onto the base assembly and have added the mid-section, rings #14 through #9, to ring #8. If you look closely at the center row of rings, you will see that I have mounted the top ring of ebony with its veneer layers and maple rings to waste blocks. Starting with ring #21, the top portion of the bowls is taking shape. I continued the process until I had joined all the rings into six bowl forms.

Once I completed the gluing work the vessels were finish-turned, sanded, and oiled. A look at **photo 12-09** shows one of the bowls ready for sanding sealer, while the other bowl awaits final turning. Note the two bottoms: the unfinished bowl still has a wide base, providing plenty of support during the shaping, while I have cut away the waste block on the finished

12-09   To maintain stability, shape the bottom of the bowls last.

bowl in order to shape its lower section.

The bowls each received six coats of finish (one coat of sanding sealer, four coats of oil, and one coat of buffed wax) while they were still mounted on the base waste block. Reverse-mounting was done as shown in Chapter 9, **photo 9.26**, so I could finish and sign the bottoms.

A big project — maybe. It depends upon your perspective. One thing is for sure, making six bowls one at a time, with 900 segments each, would have taken probably three times longer. The basic techniques used to build these bowls can be adapted to many other designs, although I am not sure I would enjoy constructing larger turnings in this manner. Frankly, I would prefer to design and build one-of-a-kind turnings, but this type of activity does help pay the bills.

If you ever decide to attempt such a project:

• Check three times before you glue anything together.

• Do not allow yourself to lose focus, which could lead to making a mistake or worse, jeopardizing safety.

• Avoid altering your saw settings until you are sure that you no longer need more pieces similarly cut. During this project I messed up the pattern on one bowl by accidentally misaligning one ring with another. Fortunately, I caught the mistake before adding more rings. I could not save the ring, but I was able to cut another 36 segments because my miter saw was still correctly set.

• Spend plenty of time planning the project, looking for shortcuts, and inventing techniques to accomplish the job as efficiently as possible.

13-06   *OVAL BOWL* #9 (5 inches tall) — reorientation of two halves creates an oval.

13.
Miscellaneous Tricks

In this chapter I will describe a few more ways to embellish a segmented turning, along with a few additional methods of construction. Once you have mastered basic construction techniques you are probably going to want to continue to challenge yourself. Some of these next techniques are risky — after many hours (or days) of work, disaster can strike and all can be lost. There are many rewards for accomplishment, while a small mistake can wipe out a large investment in time and wood. Occasional disappointment is part of the game.

Oval Bowls

Oval shapes are a nice deviation from the normal round bowl and they are not difficult to build. Special lathe equipment is not necessary, but like most segmented work, careful planning is essential. Very simply, the technique requires building a conventional taller-than-wide bowl shape, cutting it vertically into two halves, then joining the two at their top rims. **Photo 13-01** displays a turned bowl shape. The pattern on the two opposite sides of the vessel will form a completed pattern once I separate and re-join the two halves. Note the ebony segments that will later become the top edge of the finished oval bowl. I carefully laid out the shape of the bowl to duplicate one end of an oval with this particular width and length. I will later carve feet from the rim that you see protruding from the outside of the bowl, removing most of the rim in the process. While turning the vessel it was important to align the exterior profile on either side of the rim, so that a smooth surface could be created after carving away most of the rim.

Consistent wall thickness is always important, but even more so in this project. When I split

13-01   Notice the small drilled holes that can be used to check wall thickness.

the vessel apart any inconsistency will be very noticeable along the exposed edge. There are many methods and tools for measuring wall thickness, but in this case I can use an unconventional method. After determining the location of the cut line, I simply drilled a series of tiny holes, and used the depth gauge on my caliper. The holes did no harm because they disappeared when I cut the bowl in half. If you look closely at the dark ebony segments, you might be able to see my depth-gauge holes.

After completing all the turning and sanding that could be done, I cut off the waste block, drilled a few more holes at the bottom, and placed tape over the inside of the holes. I reverse-mounted the bowl and rounded the bottom using the caliper depth gauge against the tape to check wall thickness. Once you have cut the vessel apart it is too late to adjust wall thickness, except by sanding.

In **photo 13-02** (next page), for stability, I have attached the bowl to a small piece of MDF with double-sided tape, and also have applied masking tape to the desired cut line. The edge of the tape provides a nice guide for the saw

13-02   Mounting the bowl on a flat board provides stability during cutting.

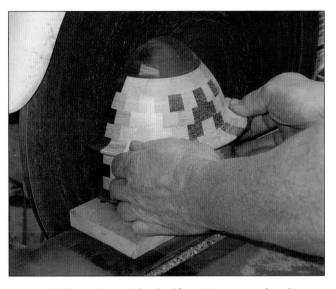

13-03   The cuts on the half-sections can be disc-sanded while still attached to the board.

13-04   To maintain this particular pattern, one layer is removed from one side.

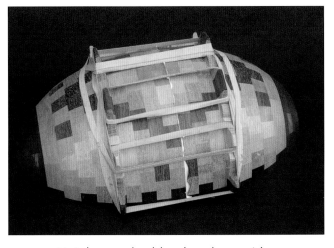

13-05   Notches and rubber bands provide an easy clamping method.

blade. Using a fine-toothed 1/2-inch blade, I split the bowl into two halves, and sanded the cuts (**photo 13-03**) before removing the halves from the MDF.

The designed pattern of colored segments contained a single center strip, therefore I needed to remove one of the half-rings from one of the half-sections. I attached one side to the MDF as shown in **photo 13-04** and cut off one layer, then sanded the cut line while the piece was still attached.

The two halves were almost ready to be glued together, but first I had to cut notches in the rim

so I could apply rubber bands as shown in **photo 13-05**. You can see the precise alignment of the two halves.

Using a combination of burr-style power-carving tools, small drill-mounted sanding discs, a palm sander, and hand sanding, I shaped the feet, cleaned up the glue seam, and sanded the top edge. The result (**photo 13-06, page 128**) is an oval bowl turned on a conventional lathe. This technique is probably the simplest example of transforming one lathe-formed shape into another. The goal was to produce an oval shape; try to imagine the other shapes that are possible by first starting

13-07 *ROCK 'N ROLLER* (16-inch diameter donuts) — a precise fit is required.

with a different shape. Think about the results of cutting an object into more than two pieces. The concept of transforming objects by cutting and reassembling presents endless possibilities. Stephen Hogbin, the well-known Canadian woodturner, has created many innovative pieces of art by realigning lathe-formed parts. If this type of work intrigues you, then check out Hogbin's work, it will open your eyes.

Mitering Complete Rings

ROCK 'N ROLLER (**photo 13-07**) required assembling tapered rings into a donut shape. The title refers to the rocking motion that results from tilting the piece on edge and releasing it on a smooth surface: because of its shape and balance, it will rock and roll for almost three minutes. The construction of the front donut is unusual. Instead of stacking rings in the conventional sense, I mitered individual rings and treated

them as segments. I considered several methods for accomplishing this task, including a jig with a router, followed by disc sanding. I had done that in order to build the outside donut ring in *MYRTLE MOONS* (**photo 8-03**). A faster, more accurate method is to miter the rings on the drum sander.

To demonstrate this unique technique I will build another *ROCK 'N ROLLER* style turning. My design for this piece is two interlocking donuts, each with a 12-inch outside diameter and 4-inch inside diameter (*ROCK 'N ROLLER* has 16-inch diameter donuts). The goal is to fit each donut through the hole of the other donut. I must build one of the donuts in two halves, which can be joined towards the end of the project. My solution to this challenge was to miter small rings into a donut shape. To start, I assembled fifty-five 4-1/2 inch diameter rings from segments that were slightly less than an inch tall. I disc-sanded both sides of the rings to

13-08   Rings are tapered using a drum sander and transport trays with a shim under one edge.

create smooth surfaces. Since they were going to be further sanded, perfect glue surfaces were not necessary. Then I used a band saw with a re-saw guide to split each ring, thus creating 110 rings about .4 inch tall. If the rings had been any smaller, for safety's sake I probably would have parted them on the lathe instead of on the band saw. To convert these small rings into segments required milling each side to a specific angle.

In **photo 13-08** I have attached a 1/8-inch shim to the underside of one edge of 3/4-inch particleboard transport trays, and I have attached the rings with their smooth sides down using a few beads of hot-melt glue. I passed the trays through the drum sander enough times to erase all the band saw marks. The shims made one side of each ring 1/8-inch thinner than the other side. I was careful to remove minimum wood from the thick side.

I removed all the rings and scraped the trays clean of hot-melt residue. The ultimate goal was to create rings whose thick and thin sides would establish the correct angle. I had no means of directly measuring the miter angle

associated with the rings, but I could accurately measure the two thicknesses. I built the rings 4.5 inches in diameter in order to have a little room for final shaping. My initial goal for the outside diameter of the donut was 12.25 inches, with an inside diameter of 3.75 inch. Using these diameters, I calculated that the circumferences were 38.5 inches and 11.785 inches respectively. My plan was to use 98 rings to create the donut, so dividing the circumferences by 98 meant that the outside and inside thicknesses of each ring needed to be .392 inch and .12 inch respectively. This is a difference of .273 inch, so I increased the thickness of the tray shims to .273 inch. I glued a second shim to the first, creating a slightly oversized thickness, then I passed the upside-down trays through the drum sander until the difference between the shimmed side and un-shimmed side was .27 inch. I did not expect to achieve a set of 98 perfectly mitered rings, but to achieve a useable set, perfection had to be the goal.

After establishing the thicker shim, I reinstalled all the rings with their tapered sides facing down. I could have done all the sanding on just one side of each ring, but I wanted an equal angle on either side. After multiple passes through the sander, my measurements indicated that the shims were a smidgen too thick. I applied two layers of masking tape under the un-shimmed side. After another pass through the sander I removed four rings, stacked them, and measured their total thickness inside and outside. Measuring four thickness and then dividing by four is more accurate than measuring just one. The measurements were close enough, so I removed all the rings from the trays. The rings, miter-sanded on both sides, are shown in **photo 13-09**. The red slash marks, which I made before removing the rings from the trays, indicate the thickest portion of each ring. Before sanding I aligned half of the rings on the trays with a segment seam positioned to the outside, and the other half with a segment center to the outside. This was important because it allowed me to assemble the rings in a brick-laying pattern without any loss of angle.

Assembling 98 mitered rings into the desired donut shape was a multi-step process. Using spring clamps I first glued together pairs. The rings were quite fragile (.12 inch thick on the thin side) and a little flexible, so to ensure adequate clamping pressure all around the glue joint I used lots of clamps, as shown in **photo 13-10**. I hung the rings as shown in order to minimize glue squeeze-out on the unglued surfaces.

Next, I very lightly disc-sanded the next set of opposing surfaces to remove any glue contamination, and assembled groups of four rings. By calipering the sectional circumference of each group of four, I determined that the outside length was slightly short, meaning that 98 rings would produce a diameter less that 12.25 inch. The solution was what woodworkers call a design change: instead of 98 rings, my donut would now contain 102 rings. The important lesson here is to measure early in the gluing process so you are not surprised when it is too late to modify your plan. I would have been out of luck had I not made a few extra rings at the beginning. I proceeded to glue up

13-09   Accuracy of the tapers depends upon minuscule shim adjustments.

13-10   Gluing the ring together starts by gluing pairs.

13-11   This is an example of creative clamping.

13-12   A large jam-chuck provides access to the inner surface.

13-13   An inner jam-chuck allows the outer surface to be worked upon.

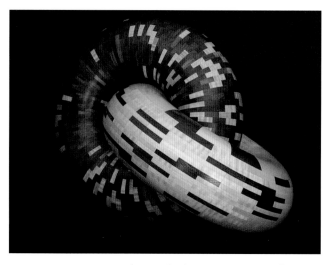

13-14   *Integration* (12-inch diameter donuts) — all the wood grain direction is consistent.

groups of eight rings. The groups of four were stiff and solid so I was able to use just two clamps, one on the inside and one on the outside. I continued to join rings in this fashion until I had assembled four quarter-sections, which I then joined into two half-sections as shown in **photo 13-11** (previous page). Creative clamping is often necessary: I used gluing cauls attached with hot-melt, and rubber bands.

Now the two halves were just about ready for turning. I touched them up on the disc sander to create a good joint and temporarily joined them with double-sided tape. The remainder of this project was relatively simple and I am not going to outline every detail. I constructed a second ring with the layers conventionally oriented, then used large outside and inside jam-chucks made from layers of MDF to turn the two rings (**photos 13-12** and **photo 13-13**).

I split the first ring apart at the taped joint and checked how it fit around the second ring. Careful measuring of the corresponding diameters and the use of a 4-inch diameter template helped create the desired fit. Before installing the two half-donuts through the other donut, I applied multiple coats of oil to all three components. Then I carefully glued the two halves in place, did a little handwork to clean up the final seam, and applied finish oil. The finished turning, *Integration*, is shown in **photo 13-14**.

Building the first donut in this project is a good example of unconventional problem solving: the challenge was how to miter completed rings. For me, one of the biggest joys of segmented work is inventing techniques. As your designs become more complex, that old expression, "Necessity is the mother of invention," certainly applies.

This technique for mitering complete rings is not restricted to building donut shapes. Another example is a turning called *Growth*, shown in **photo 13-15**. In this piece the rings vary in diameter and the miter angles gradually change to create the desired curvature. Assembly of this shape was also different: the rings are not only tapered, but their outside and inside surfaces

13-16   *TALKING WITH WOOD* (16 inches diameter) — inserting round elements can be tricky.

13-15   *GROWTH* (27 inches tall) — another example of using tapered complete rings.

were also individually turned and finished before assembly. Gluing the rings together would have unavoidably resulted in glue squeeze-out, something I did not want to have to clean out of all those little valleys. My solution was to attach each ring individually to its neighbor with small wood screws. It was a time-consuming chore, but preferable to dealing with glue squeeze-out.

Installing Round Designs

As segmented turners we deal with things in the round, but most of the components that we assemble have straight edges. This is not always the case. Instead of building a feature ring to decorate a turning, objects can be modified by cutting openings and installing round decorative plugs. The vessel *TALKING WITH WOOD* (**photo 13-16**) is one such example. Its top surface contains three Indian faces that I constructed as plugs and then inserted into turned holes. I have experimented with router jigs for making round holes, but to achieve the best results the hole needs to be slightly tapered, not easy to rout into a curved surface. Cutting the holes on the lathe is the alternative and it can be a tricky and time-consuming job.

13-17   Off-center turning requires a large counter-balanced disc.

13-18   Secure and accurate positioning is required.

13-19   This is not a time for aggressive wood removal.

TALKING WITH WOOD is approximately 16 inches in diameter, and offset-mounting the top portion was necessary to cut the openings. I used a 30-inch diameter disk of 1-inch MDF as my mounting surface (**photo 13-17**). Attached to the MDF you can see a counterweight in the form of a heavy 8-inch faceplate on one side and three sloped pieces of MDF on the other side. The top portion of the turning was temporarily glued to a 16-inch circle of MDF using hot-melt and then, using a single centered screw, I attached this assembly to the center sloped piece of MDF (you can see the screw hole in **photo 13-17**). The angle of the sloped pieces positioned the curved section of the turning at a right angle to the lathe spindle. To improve the attachment of the assembly, in addition to the center screw I applied a few beads of hot-melt glue to the underside seams. In **photo 13-18** you can see the centered screw under the right side of the tool rest. This screw not only held the assembly in place, but also enabled me to rotate the assembly to the next position. After fitting a plug I only had to loosen the screw, cut the hot melt beads, and rotate to the next opening position. **Photo 13-18** shows the start of the first hole. **Photo 13-19** shows the assembly spinning

13-20   Multiple test-fitting attempts are usually necessary.

on the lathe while I cut an opening (I am trying to not block the camera view), and **photo 13-20** shows the second opening ready for its plug. I fit the plugs as described in Chapter 7. As you can imagine, a lot of work went into constructing the turning prior to this particular step. I really did not want to see anything go wrong and it was a relief to successfully complete the operation.

An easier method of inserting plugs into a vessel surface is described towards the end of the next chapter.

14-04   *COSMOS WITH SATELLITE BOXES* (36 inches tall(— can you find the icosahedrons?

14.
Building an Icosahedron

If you are like most people, you are probably saying to yourself, "What the heck is an icosahedron?" Well, believe it or not, there have been many books written on the subject. An icosahedron is one of five Platonic solids, which are regular three-dimensional solids constructed from regular and identical two-dimensional polygons. The most familiar Platonic solid is the cube, which has six identical square sides. The icosahedron consists of 20 identical equilateral triangles. My focus here is to demonstrate a construction process.

At the time I did not know the form's name nor that its origin went back to the time of the Greek scholar Plato, but I constructed my first 20-faceted sphere in 1980 as a learning toy for my infant son, Andy. This was long before I became interested in lathe turning, I just thought it was a clever woodworking project. I recall seeing a plastic version in a toy store and thinking that I could build one of wood. I later discovered that the form is called an icosahedron. Somehow that toy has survived the play of two kids and numerous family pets; I show it to you in **photo 14-01**.

Years later it occurred to me that I could turn this type of form into a spherical shape and use it in my wood art projects. Near the front of this book there is a photo of *ALICE'S GARDEN* (**photo 1.01**). I attached 12 trumpet shapes to a sphere to create this turning. The icosahedron's configuration of 20 triangles creates 12 intersections of 5 triangular points, thus the decision to attach 12 shapes to the sphere. **Photo 14-02** shows a close-up interior view of this 20-sided sphere. Another example of using the icosahedron spherical design is *THE JUGGLER* (**photo 14-03**); again, I attached 12 shapes to a centrally positioned sphere.

14-01   *ANDY'S TOY* (9 in. dia.) — my first icosahedron.

14-02   *ALICE'S GARDEN* — interior view showing an icosahedron-turned sphere.

14-03   *THE JUGGLER* — another example of an icosahedron-turned sphere.

14-05   An icosahedron is composed of 20 mitered triangles.

14-06   Triangle edges can be mitered using a table saw jig with a hold-down clamp..

The use of this spherical design is not limited to anchoring other elements. I have also built vessel forms and many small boxes using this type of construction. *Cosmos*, pictured in **photo 14-04** (page 138) contains a free-spinning icosahedron at its center and the small boxes in the foreground are also constructed from mitered triangles. Jack Cox's book, *Beyond Basic Turning* (Linden Publishing), offers several projects using Platonic solids. I only wish that I had discovered this fascinating book years ago when it was first published.

The key to successfully constructing this type of sphere is two-fold: the miters have to be precise, and the gluing/clamping operation must be accurate. I have found that an all-at-one-time gluing technique works best. To attempt gluing 20 mitered triangles together one at a time presents too many opportunities for cumulative errors. Gluing all 20 triangles at the same time is no easy task either, but I have successfully done it many times.

The first questions that arise are: what miter angle to use on the triangles, and what size to cut them? By trial and error, I found the miter angle is approximately 21°, I later discovered that the exact angle is 20.905°. The approximate finished diameter of a sphere built in this manner will be less than twice a triangle side length. This is a rough estimate and does not include any consideration for splines placed between the triangles. Another factor is the thickness of the wood. For spheres up to about 8 inches in diameter, 3/4-inch thick material is adequate. If you attempt a larger shape, the curvature of the turned sphere will likely require thicker wood.

Here is my method for building a 20-sided sphere using mitered triangles:

The first step is to cut the triangles. I have done this several ways and have determined that a two-step approach works best. Set your miter saw (or table saw) at 30° and cut three triangles from scrap material. Place them together and check to see if they form a straight 180° line, and adjust your saw until they do. Then, cut six triangles, clamp them into a ring, and check the accuracy again. It helps to sand off the inside points a little, to avoid the challenge of aligning six points.

After you have adjusted your saw, cut 20 triangles (**photo 14-05**). These are not compound-miter cuts, but the triangle sides must be equal in length. If the lengths are all equal, then the angles have to be equal. Another quick method of checking the accuracy is to select random pairs of triangles and position them on top of each other. Rotate them and examine the match of the three sides, they should match every which way.

14-07   Masking tape holds pieces in alignment.

14-08   Fold the pieces and double check the accuracy of the fit.

Cut 15 extra triangles the same size from MDF, to use later as test pieces (**photo 14-05**).

The easiest and most accurate method of mitering the triangle sides is to use a small sled on the table saw. I have used a larger sled such as the one for the compound miters in Chapter 10, but in this situation the smaller sled works better. **Photo 14-06** shows my device. It is just a piece of MDF with two angled pieces of MDF mounted on top to create a 60° trap for the triangles, and a toggle-style clamp to securely lock the triangles in place. The 60° trap must be dead-on. Cut the two angled pieces of MDF with the same setting that you used to cut the triangles.

The mathematicians say the miter angle is 21.905°, so that is the ideal blade angle to set. Make your best guess setting this blade angle and cut just one side of five test pieces. Before making all five cuts, confirm the accuracy of the jig trap by making a few cuts that only remove a portion of the triangle edge and examine the alignment of these cuts with the top edge of the triangle. Is the cut parallel to the side of the triangle? After cutting one side from five pieces, adjust your fence towards the blade just a smidgen and cut one more side from the same five pieces of scrap.

Sand the point off the corner of the miter cuts. This will ease the task of fitting them together.

Place the five pieces on a flat surface and tape them together as shown in the bottom of **photo 14-07**. Roll the pieces together to form a cone shape and apply one more piece of tape to hold them together, as shown on the left side of **photo 14-08**. Closely examine the joints. Close is not good enough, they have to be perfect. Adjust the saw as necessary and test again until you have achieved the proper fit. To confirm the fit cut ten identical pieces, assemble them into a straight line as shown in the top of **photo 14-07**, and roll them into a ring as shown on the right of **photo 14-08**.

You can now proceed to cut the good stuff. Cut only one side from each triangle, followed by a slight adjustment of the fence towards the blade before cutting the next side, and so forth. The exact amount of wood removed from each triangle side makes little difference. If the cutting-sled trap-angle is accurate, then one cut effectively shortens all three sides equally. How does one cut shorten all three sides? Look at a triangle: one cut shortens two sides and creates a new, shorter third side. The reason for adjusting the fence inward after each series of cuts is just to make sure that you make a complete cut and don't leave a flat, uncut spot at the top of the side.

Precise assembly of 20 triangles with 30 matching sides and 12 perfectly matched intersections of 5 points is well beyond my

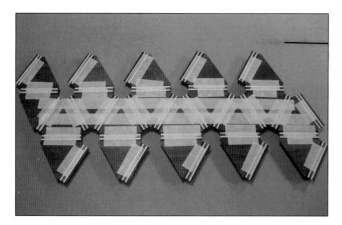

14-09   This can be folded into a sphere.

14-10   Gluing requires quickness and maybe a little luck.

14-11   The six hose clamps have been reinstalled for ease of viewing.

ability, I am not even tempted to try it. Sure, the 20 pieces can be glued together, but tiny mismatches at the point intersections will ruin the appearance. By installing a spline at each seam, I can dramatically improve my chances of success. The splines will create openings at each of the 12 intersections of points, thus hiding minor misalignments. The the splines can also dilute any inaccuracy in the final fit. If there's a tiny gap between two triangle miters, then adding a spline should divide that gap into two smaller gaps and reduce its likelihood of detection. The splines do add another element to the gluing challenge. The thickness and choice of spline material is completely up to you, the only requirement is that the splines have parallel sides. In the example that I am describing, I laminated five narrow strips of wood — two of wenge, two of maple, and one of purpleheart. A single strip just as easily could have been used.

The biggest challenge is the actual gluing operation. It requires taping the entire assembly together as shown in **photo 14-09**. This photo shows that all the wood grain in all of the triangles is oriented the same horizontal direction. While the splines do present a small compromise, there are no perpendicular alignments. The least desirable joints are still at an angle to each other. Later, when I insert plugs at the intersections, the lengths of these joints will be reduced. After taking this photo I applied a second layer of duct tape to the assembly to improve the holding power (**photo 14-10**). This assembly was very floppy and difficult to handle. To flip it over, I placed another board on top and flipped both layers with the taped pieces in between.

Now for the real fun, you need to perform a dry-fit with hose clamps. I highly recommend enlisting the help of another pair of hands. I can maneuver small sizes without help, but spheres of this size are too cumbersome to control alone. It helps to place the pieces into a circular hollow such as a rough-turned bowl during dry-fitting and gluing — the circular rim acts as another pair of hands. The arrangement of triangles determines the positioning of the hose clamps.

Six different alignments accommodate the placement of a clamp around the form's circumference. These six circumferences avoid the pointed intersections and provide the most effective clamping pressure. I took a photo of the glued form, but unfortunately, squeezed-out foam from Gorilla Glue obscured the view. I have to warn you that gluing a sphere of this size is a very messy affair. To give you a better view, I reinstalled the clamps around the cleaned-up sphere (**photo 14-11**).

Even with slow-setting glue, time is critical. Gather all tools, clamps, rubber gloves, spreading devices. Talk about the procedure with your assistant. Polyurethane is the best choice of glue because it gives you the longest slippery working time and because it is not necessary to meticulously coat both surfaces of each glue joint. One surface is enough, which saves time. As you apply the hose clamps, it is important that the joints remain slippery so they will slide into place. It is also important that you tighten the clamps very methodically, as you would tighten lug nuts on a wheel, while checking and adjusting the alignment of all the components. If a component such as a spline slips inward, use a screwdriver though one of the openings to realign it as necessary. This is a nerve-wracking procedure requiring quickness, teamwork, and maybe a little luck. You might want to consider gaining a little experience by constructing a smaller sphere before attempting one this size.

After the glue has cured the next step is to sand the exterior glue seams and check the tightness of the joints. I used a large, 7-inch handheld disc sander with coarse grit to clean the surface and expose all the seams. If a poor joint is discovered, there is little that can be done to salvage the sphere, though perhaps a section could be transformed into an open bowl. Before spending time at the lathe, I like to confirm the appearance of all the seams. An icosahedron is quite a challenge and unfortunately, most viewers have no appreciation for the accomplishment though occasionally an experienced woodworker comes along and expresses his admiration.

If you are intrigued by Platonic and Archimedian solids, two books, *Spherical Models* and *Polyhedron Models*, both by Magnus J. Wenninger, offer dozens of designs. Most of Wenninger's paper models are probably too complex to be adapted to wood construction, but for anyone looking for the ultimate woodworking challenge, I recommend his intriguing volumes. Another mathematician, George Hart, has done an incredible amount of work with spherical forms and has an amazing web site devoted to this subject. I highly recommend a visit to both of their web sites at www.georgehart.com and http://employees.csbsju.edu/mwenninger.

Sphere Turning Techniques

I usually do the rough-turning of a sphere with the aid of a tailstock. Unfortunately, I was still waiting for a back-ordered tailstock assembly for a new lathe, so I had to shape this sphere another way. Normally I would use a large cup-style drive to hold one end, with a live center carrying another smaller cup at the other end. By mounting the form between the two cups in a variety of positions I can turn the shape in multiple directions, resulting in a very round sphere. Without a tailstock, this is how I accomplished transforming the icosahedron into a round sphere.

I glued a 3-inch disc of maple to one of the flat triangular surfaces and used this to lathe-mount the sphere in a four-jaw chuck as shown in **photo 14-12** (next page). A faceplate-mounted waste block would have also worked. Notice that I did not use a circle of MDF. Without penetrating screws, the MDF by itself is not strong enough.

My initial focus with my gouge was to eliminate all the high ridges and flat spots in order to determine the likely finished diameter. After achieving a fairly round form I measured the diameter using two squares, also shown in **photo 14-12**, and then used the 7-1/4 inch dimension to create a template, which I lathe-cut from 3/4-inch MDF. While frequently checking the sphere with the template, I

14-12   A glued waste block permits rough shaping.

14-13   A thin, turned ring makes an effective template.

14-14   A Large jam chuck with keeper ring secures the sphere.

proceeded to create a smooth round surface. Turning a sphere in this manner is not as quick, easy, or accurate as turning between centers in multiple directions, but I managed to accomplish the task. **Photo 14-13** shows the outward portion of the sphere with templates positioned against its surface.

At this point I built a large jam-chuck with a retaining ring and mounted the sphere with the maple waste block facing outward, as shown in **photo 14-14**. This jam-chuck is simply a hollow form built from layers of MDF, with its inside diameter turned to snugly fit the outside of the sphere. The jam-chuck only makes contact with the sphere at its outside rim. I bolted the retaining ring onto the chuck without the sphere in place and turned an opening that would secure the sphere. Then I secured the sphere using carriage bolts, whose rounded heads made things a little safer.

If you have a copy of David Springett's book, *Woodturning Wizardry*, take a look at his use of jam-chucks with retaining rings. He executes some very intricate sphere modifications using smaller versions of this type of containment device. If you happen to see his book in a bookstore, there is actually a photo on the front cover of a small jam-chuck with retaining ring.

Using a section of the template, I shaped one end of the sphere. Repeated repositioning and turning within the jam-chuck would have resulted in a more perfect form, but I chose to first insert plugs at the intersections.

I made the plugs before cutting the plug holes. The two-piece plugs consisted of a ring of 10 wenge segments around a center piece of solid bird's-eye maple. I mounted the wenge rings to small MDF circles using hot-melt glue and then attached band-sawn circles of maple to the wenge, as shown on the left side of **photo 14-15**. By lathe-mounting the MDF circle in a four-jaw chuck, I could first turn the maple plug, followed by the wenge plug. I used a caliper to size the plug diameters approximately 1.9 inches and 2.4 inches respectively. By accurately sizing the plugs, I only had to turn the holes to fit. If the plugs fit, then consistency was automatic.

A tricky part of inserting the plugs is accurately positioning the sphere within the jam-chuck. This requires a little trial-and-error. By cutting an undersized opening, you can compare the spacing between the splines. If they are not equal then reposition the sphere accordingly before turning the opening to the required diameter. **Photo 14-16** shows that the jarrah wood dimension between the splines on the right side is less than on the left side. By placing a dowel into the hole and giving it a leftwards hammer-tap, the centering is improved. By tapping, turning, and checking a few times, equal spacing can be achieved.

After centering the opening it was a matter of tightening the nuts one last time to firmly secure the sphere and then turning the opening to fit the wenge plug (see plug fitting in Chapter 7). Without taking the assembly off the lathe, I glued the wenge plug into place and then worked on something else while the glue cured. Ten minutes is plenty of waiting time for small plugs such as these.

The maple plug hole was then turned inside the wenge plug and that plug was glued into place. Before repositioning the sphere, I used a section of my template to make sure the plugs did not protrude, so they wouldn't interfere with the jam-chuck fit. I also turned a tiny indentation into the center of the maple plug and used this to drill a small centered hole using a drill press. These small holes would later be used to attach other spheres to the icosahedron. **Photo 14-17** shows a close-up of a few of the installed plugs, before finish-turning the surface. I repeated the process until all 12 openings were plugged.

Using the same jam-chuck I turned the sphere, repositioned it, turned it some more, and so forth, and then sanded the surface. Before sanding I enlarged the jam-chuck opening slightly and glued a few small pieces of rubber pad to its inside rim in order to avoid marring the sphere. I did not use the retaining ring, but instead, I just kept one hand in contact with the sphere while the lathe turned and used the other hand to operate a 3-inch disc sander.

This particular sphere became the center of a

14-15   Install all the components of the plug before relocating the sphere to the next location.

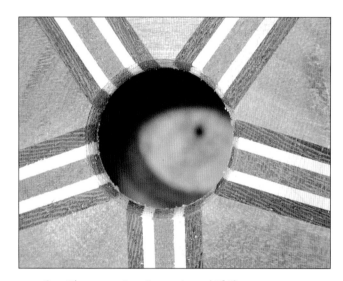

14-16   The opening is centered if the space between splines is equal.

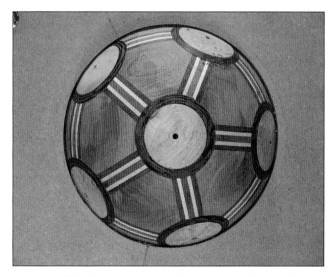

14-17   All of the openings have been plugged.

14-18   *PLATONIC MOLECULE* (28 inches tall) —- a small tribute to Plato.

sculptural piece that I titled *PLATONIC MOLECULE* (in honor of Plato), as shown in **photo 14-18**.

The remainder of the project consisted of creating the smaller spheres and building the base. The only other noteworthy technique pertains to constructing the 3-inch spheres with their orbit-like rings. These were first assembled by stacking five segmented rings using the MDF disc/carriage bolt technique that I described in Chapters 7 and 12. To create the thin contrasting stripes at assorted angles, I turned the stacks of rings into spheres by first using a four-jaw chuck on my large lathe and then a cup drive/cup live center combination on my mini-lathe. **Photos 14-19** and **14-20** show the two different lathe mountings. **Photo 14-19** shows the assembly of rings mounted directly into the four-jaw chuck without any waste block, which was possible because most of this portion would be turned off in the next step. Using a template, I rough-turned one side of each assembly round on the large lathe and then transferred it to the mini-lathe in order to use its tailstock. After rounding the other end, I used a small cup center in conjunction with the live tailstock to turn the sphere in several positions, as shown in **photo 14-20**.

Once I had achieved a fairly round form I positioned the spheres to make a scoring cut, as also shown in **photo 14-20**. I then used this shallow parting-tool groove as my guide to saw the spheres in half on the band saw. **Photos 14-21** and **14-22** show the sequential steps. I used the applied tabs of duct tape as handles while cutting and disc-sanding. It was a matter of repeatedly cutting the sphere apart, disc-sanding the cuts smooth, gluing a ring of bloodwood segments to one side, sanding the bloodwood ring, and then joining the two halves back together. The bloodwood segments were treated as thick veneer. The strips that they were cut from had been accurately dimensioned and sanded and the segments taped together. At the top of **photo 14-21**, a bloodwood ring is being glued to one-half of a sphere, using piece of dense 1/8-inch thick foam rubber between the bloodwood segments and

14-19   Turning a stack of rings into a sphere.

14-20   The tailstock holds a sphere as it is split with a parting tool.

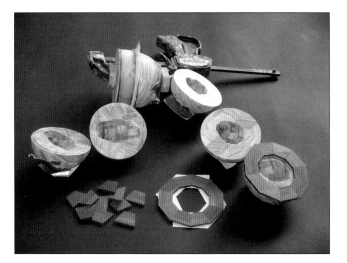

14-21   The sphere's diameter is maintained because the ring thickness equals the kerf.

14-22   These spheres are in various stages of construction.

the circle of flat MDF. With the assistance of the rubber pad, the clamping pressure creates a tight bond with the individual segments. The piece of wax paper in the photo simply prevented glue contact with the rubber pad. On the right of **photo 14-21** you can see the results of this gluing step. The next step was to sand the bloodwood circumference to match the canarywood, smooth the gluing surface, and then join the halves back together. **Photo 14-22** shows a few examples of the various steps. In total, twelve spheres were cut in half at least four times each and two separate gluing steps were required to rejoin them each time. In order to keep the spheres fairly round, the thickness

of the inserted ring needed to closely match the saw-kerf that had been removed. By matching these two dimensions, it was also possible to maintain the alignment of the original horizontal layers.

To create a smooth sanded surface I made a small modified jam-chuck, as seen in **photo 14-23** (next page). This jam-chuck was simply two layers of 1-inch MDF mounted into a four-jaw chuck and turned to fit the diameter of the spheres. Instead of turning a tight fit, I enlarged the opening and glued three small pieces of 1/8-inch dense foam rubber to the contacting edge of the jam-chuck. This allowed me to quickly re-position the spheres during sanding.

14-23   A small jam-chuck (and fingers) holds the spheres during sanding.

I used a relatively slow lathe speed (about 350 rpm) and made sure the sphere would not become dislodged by keeping a couple of fingers in contact with it while sanding. I was quite amused when I viewed **photo 14-23** and noticed that my little finger had been extended well out of the way of the four-jaw chuck. This may appear dangerous, after all, there are two risks: the spinning chuck, and the spinning sanding disc. Sometimes a little danger is a good thing, it keeps you alert. As with all sanding, be careful not to overdo it. With such a small item it only takes a few seconds of sanding with each grit to erase the scratch marks from the previous grit.

The remainder of the project required creating the smaller spheres and the base unit. To securely attach the spheres, I used small steel threaded dowels. If you are not familiar with this type of hardware, they look like double-ended wood screws with no head. One end is screwed into one component using locking pliers, then the other component can be screwed onto the other end. Glued wooden dowels would have worked, but the threaded steel dowels are superior.

Transforming Spheres into Vessels

The technique of inserting an angled ring into a sphere is not limited to small spheres or small rings. A few years ago, when senator/astronaut John Glenn went up on the space shuttle, I made a turning (**photo 14-24**) to commemorate the event — I have always been a fan of the space program. I delivered it to a San Francisco gallery on the day that Sen. Glenn's picture appeared on the cover of Time magazine and it sold immediately. The turning, *FOR JOHN GLENN*, with its three orbits representing Sen. Glenn's space flight, is an example of two techniques: inserting angled rings into a sphere, and transforming a sphere into a vessel. The rings in this turning are not just thin layers of one wood, they are multi-laminations. To maintain the alignment of the horizontal layers, I removed an exact thickness of material to match the thickness of each inserted ring. The same basic technique that was used to make the previous small spheres was used for this large, 14-inch sphere. After installing the three rings, it was relatively simple to replace the top and bottom portions using a large jam-chuck with retaining ring as my lathe-mounting method.

By using a jam-chuck with a retaining ring, many modifications can be done to a sphere. Decorating a sphere with plugs and then transforming the sphere into something else is another method for solving a design challenge. The vessel, *24 HOUR PITCHER* (**photo 14-25,** page 150), is a good example of this technique. The center portion of the vessel started out as a sphere, which I could easily position within a large lathe-mounted containment device. The title refers to the four designs, which show four different time of day scenes. The scenes were created using marquetry techniques with 3/4-inch wood. I built four large plugs, which I then fit into large turned holes in the sphere. After I finished the sphere modifications using the jam-chuck, I removed the lower portion of the sphere and glued it to the base section. Then I removed the top portion of the sphere and added the vessel top. Inserting plugs into a sphere is much easier than trying to insert

14-24 *FOR JOHN GLENN* (14 inches diameter) — a larger example of angled rings.

them into a finalized vessel shape. Of course, to ensure a smooth profile transition, a detailed blueprint is essential.

Another example of converting a sphere into a vessel is *MIDNIGHT SNOW* (**photo 14-26,** page 150). This turning also began as a sphere, allowing me to reposition it to install randomly spaced snowflake-style plugs. The snowflakes were created using disc-sander techniques and then turned into round plugs. The darkness of the ebony effectively hides the plug glue lines.

A Truncated Icosahedron

Constructing forms such as an icosahedron will challenge all of your woodworking skills. The icosahedron is just one of many possible spherical forms that await your saw blade. There are many complicated forms that use a combination of shapes. A soccer ball is a common example, with its arrangement of pentagons (five-sided) and hexagons (six-sided).

Many years ago I did a series of turnings I called my sports bowl series. Three of those turnings

14-25   *24 HOUR PITCHER* (20 in. tall)— the pictures were inserted into a sphere as large plugs.

14-26   *MIDNIGHT SNOW* (17 in.) — the snowflakes were built as plugs and inserted into a sphere.

are shown in **photo 14-27**. This was both a fun and challenging project. All the balls were made as bowls approximately the size of actual sports balls. In the photo, from left to right, the titles are, *FOOTBOWL, SOCCER BOWL,* and *BOWL 'N BALL.* I include them here to talk about the *SOCCER BOWL,* by far the most difficult piece in the series. A soccer ball is made from 20 hexagons and 12 pentagons. In the world of geometry the form is called a truncated icosahedron, to truncate is to cut off a section of a shape. Look at the soccer ball and imagine the six-sided sections as triangles with their three corners cut off by the pentagon sections. When I made it I had glued together many icosahedrons, but this challenge had me scratching my head for several days. Instead of trying to assemble 32 mitered pieces

with 60 precisely aligned intersections of points, my solution was to build the icosahedron first, using yellowheart triangles with ebony splines. The splines created a gap at each of the 12 intersections of triangular points. The challenge was to insert pentagon shapes at these 12 locations. My solution was to create round plugs that contained the five-sided shapes surrounded by matching ebony strips. The pentagons that you see are actually round plugs fitted just as previously described, using a large jam-chuck with a retaining ring. I discovered one of these plugs in my box of leftovers. To help you visualize the technique I show it to you in **photo 14-28**.

I secured the main sphere in a large jam-chuck with a retaining ring, centered each location,

14-27   *SPORTS BOWLS — FOOTBOWL, SOCCER BOWL,* and *BOWL 'N BALL* (life size).

and turned the recess to fit a plug. The trick was to align the five points of the pentagons with the five splines that radiated from each hole. It worked and was a lot easier than trying to fit mitered pentagons between mitered hexagons. The top of the form (the bowl portion) was initially part of the sphere. It was parted off, turned inside-out, and then re-attached to the sphere with a ring of ebony to fill the parting tool kerf. Solutions to challenges do exist, they just have to be discovered.

14-28   The *SOCCER BOWL* pentagons were installed as plugs.

15-00   *BROKEN SPIRITS* (30 inches tall).

15.

Portholes and Large Turnings

The vessel **BROKEN SPIRITS** was constructed in three different sections, almost like three separate turnings, which I eventually joined into one vessel. The middle portion is composed of a large ring of porthole-style segments with smaller feature rings above and below. To start the project, I constructed the portholes from laminations with the Indian faces sandwiched between layers. I introduced my first turning with portholes in 1995 at an AAW symposium at Davis, California. Since then, this feature has become one of my most popular design elements. The technique involves creating designs, gluing them between layers, transforming the laminations into segments, and turning the individual porthole indentations before gluing the ring together. A side view, **photo 15-01**, shows the composition of the laminated segments.

Building a Porthole-Style Ring

The following steps outline the procedures that I used to build this porthole ring:

I first constructed the mosaic Indian face designs using a disc sander to fit all the components together. This was not difficult but it was quite a time-consuming, one-step-at-time chore. I did not follow a precise plan for each face, but designed them as I assembled the components. I started with an assortment of 3/4-inch thick scraps of wood, but ended with about 1/2-inch thick squares because there were so many sanding steps. To help determine the position of the faces within the portholes, I used a template during their construction, a 4-1/2 inch square piece of MDF, with a 3-inch centered

15-01   This is a six-layer laminated segment containing a mosaic Indian face design.

hole. During the gluing steps I frequently used the template to ensure that I had properly centered my designs and to predetermine which portion of the design would be revealed after turning the indentation. When creating this type of mosaic design, creative clamping techniques are often necessary. I used rubber bands, an assortment of clamps, and an occasional gluing caul to achieve the needed pressure alignments. I have built many porthole-style rings, but this was the first to incorporate Indian faces. My past designs had been simple landscapes built using band-saw marquetry techniques.

My ring design consisted of 16 portholes. I built eight faces, each about 4-1/2 inches square, with the intention of splitting them to create 16 designs. After completing the 8 faces, I squared them and then used my disc sander to smooth one surface of each.

For the inside (bottom) layer of each segment lamination, I milled two 4-1/2 inch wide boards of mesquite about 1/2 inch thick and 48 inches long. I glued the 8 face squares smooth side down to one of these boards of mesquite. I used a 1/4-inch piece of wood as a spacer to uniformly separate the face squares on the mesquite board, creating a saw kerf location for later cutting.

After the glue cured I passed the assembly through my drum sander until the exposed face

15-02   These are all the components that compose the laminated segment.

15-03   It pays to have lots of clamps.

surfaces were smooth with a consistent thickness of about 1/2 inch.

I glued the other board of mesquite onto the sanded face surfaces, sandwiching the mosaic faces.

After cleaning up glue squeeze-out and squaring the lamination edges of the mesquite boards, I split the faces by making two rip cuts on the table saw with the lamination on edge. This resulted in the two strips that you can see in **photo 15-02**. If you compare the two rows of faces, you will see mirror images.

I again used the drum sander to flatten and smooth the 16 exposed face surfaces. Their final thickness was slightly more than 1/8 inch.

Photo 15-02 also shows the other lamination components: in front of the face strips you can see square rings of purpleheart and maple segments. I initially glued these together as 3/4-inch thick round rings, disc-sanded them smooth, then squared and split them on a table saw. The resulting 16 thin, square rings therefore possessed one smooth, ready-to-glue surface.

Photo 15-02 also shows a stack of 32 maple veneer squares, which I later glued to either side of the purpleheart/maple layers within the lamination. The 16 squares of jarrah, which will become the outside (top) layers of the laminations, are shown in the bottom right of the photo. Before cutting the individual squares I machined the jarrah boards to a 1/2-inch thickness with a smooth drum-sanded surface ready for gluing.

Assembling the six layers (**photo 15-01**) required three steps. The first step was the previous attachment of the faces to the mesquite boards. The next step was to glue one layer of veneer and the purpleheart/maple layers to the faces. I did this using at least six spring clamps per square, as in **photo 15-03**. The top layer of purpleheart/maple presses the veneer, but in this case the segmented ring has a large center hole, and therefore the center of the veneer layer had no clamping pressure applied. Veneer that is glue-moistened and not clamped will

15-04 The circle of MDF is attached with hot-melt glue.

15-05 Do not turn too deep, the design is only 1/8-inch thick.

bubble and distort. To provide for stress relief and glue escape, I drilled a 3/4-inch centered hole in the veneer squares prior to gluing. The inside center portion of the veneer squares would be cut away later, but I did not want distortion to affect the outside glue joint.

Before adding the second layer of veneer and the jarrah squares, I passed the assemblies through the drum sander to flatten and smooth the purpleheart/maple surfaces. I reduced their thickness to slightly less than 1/8 inch.

At this point there was no longer a reason to keep the strips intact. I therefore crosscut the individual squares from the two strips. This improved clamping access during the next gluing step.

To complete the lamination process I glued on the second layer of veneer and the top layer of jarrah. After adding the faces I had marked the bottom of the mesquite squares with a centerline that I could later use to assist centering on the lathe.

After a little disc sanding and table saw work, I had 16 squares ready to have portholes turned into them. I could have mitered the sides of the squares before turning the portholes, but in case a mishap occurred, I wanted the ability to reject

one or two. By waiting until after I had finished the portholes, I kept my options open. I also needed to create a spline element to position between the finished porthole segments. This would take some time and I did not want the mitered segment-ends to age. The glue surface includes numerous pieces of oily wood end-grain, and more reliable joints result when there is little delay between cutting and gluing.

One challenge was to maintain the centering of the faces within the turned portholes. After squaring the laminated pieces, I used the previously applied centerline to hot-melt glue 3-inch MDF circles to the mesquite side of each square. The MDF circles could then be held in a four-jaw chuck to lathe-mount the segments (**photo 15-04**). Once I had partially exposed the faces during turning, I checked the centering and in a few cases repositioned the MDF circle before completing the porthole.

The actual turning (**photo 15-05**) was the quickest and easiest part of the ring construction. I turned the openings with a 1/2-inch bowl gouge and a small-radius round scraper for the inside corner. I removed a minimum of wood from the face layers and attempted to create consistently dimensioned portholes. Before removing each square from

15-06   While the arrows point vertically, the wood grain in the splines is positioned horizontally to match the adjoining segments.

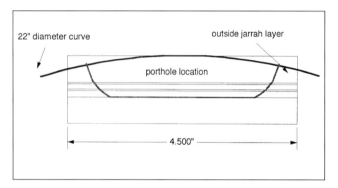

15-07   The outer layer must be thick enough for the outside vessel profile.

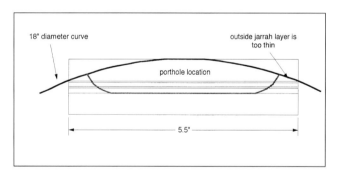

15-08   If the outer layer is too thin, inner layers will be exposed.

the chuck, I power-sanded the openings to 400-grit and applied a coat of sanding sealer.

Over the course of several days I repeatedly used the MDF circles to lathe-mount the segments so I could apply and buff numerous coats of oil finish to the portholes. I could have done this after assembling the ring, but it was

quicker and easier to use the lathe's rotation.

For a spline between the segments, I created a broken arrow design. This associated a little symbolism with the vessel title, *BROKEN SPIRITS*. Splines are not necessary, but they do nicely frame the portholes. Since these splines are more than 4-1/2 inches long, the grain direction had to match that of the horizontal segments. I began by crosscutting narrow strips of maple and mesquite and laminating them together with the grain direction oriented sideways, not lengthwise.

Much like building a zigzag ring (Chapter 11), I angle-cut and reassembled the spline material to form the broken arrow design. Instead of gluing the angled pieces together as in a conventional zigzag, I positioned a narrow piece of mesquite between each section to separate the maple sections (the arrow). At one end I added a triangular point and at the other end, I added a couple of simple feather shapes. These splines are shown in **photo 15-06**. Note that the wood grain is either horizontal or slightly angled, but not vertical, which would have positioned it at a right angle to the grain of the large segments. To ensure that the spline sides were parallel I hot-glued them to an MDF transport tray and passed them through the drum sander.

I mentioned at the beginning of this discussion the need to keep your options open for as long as possible. Well, as luck would have it, while turning/sanding one of the portholes I went through the mosaic face layer. Instead of making a replacement, I decided to reduce the number of faces from the original 16 to 14. This of course reduced the diameter, which in turn increased the sharpness of the outside curve. Before making the decision to build the ring with just 14 portholes, I drew the curve and overlaid the segment profile to confirm that the turning would not remove too much material and expose the underlying layer. This is important to understand: if the segment outer layer is too thin, or the curve too sharp, then the second layer will be exposed at the glue joints. A couple of simple drawings (**photos 15-07** and **15-08**) show the difference between acceptable

15-09   A table saw sled results in a smoother cut.

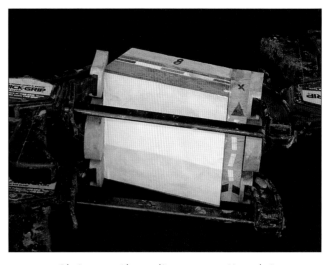

15-10   Gluing on the splines saves time later.

and disaster. The layout in **photo 15-07** displays my actual laminated porthole segment with the predicted outside curve of the vessel. As you can see, there is enough wood thickness on either side of the porthole. The layout in **photo 15-08** shows what would happen if the outside curve were sharper and/or the segments were wider. Shaping the vessel's outside surface would expose the second layer within the lamination and probably would ruin the appearance.

With the splines completed and the portholes oiled, the next step was to miter the segments. I used the table saw with a crosscut blade and a small sled to make the 12.86° segment-end miter cuts (360° divided by 28 angles). Several series of test cuts using 1-inch MDF were necessary to set the correct blade angle. **Photo 15-09** displays a miter cut in progress. The small square of MDF on top of the segment provides a contact point for the hold-down clamp. After cutting both sides I examined the centering of each porthole within its segment, adjusted the table fence slightly towards the blade, and trimmed a little off whichever side was longest.

You might be wondering why I used a sled to cut the miters instead of just sliding the segments along the table and fence — the segments were certainly large enough to handle safely. A sled built from three layers of MDF has weight, which dampens vibration. It also provides a smooth ride over the table-saw

insert, which otherwise could cause tiny inconsistencies. The result is a smoother crosscut on the end-grain of the segment.

I dry-fit the 14 segments and confirmed the accuracy of the fit. To protect the porthole surfaces, before any gluing I covered the openings with masking tape.

Instead of an all-at-one-time glue job, I first glued one spline to one side of each segment (**photo 15-10**). This reduced the total number of components, simplifying the job. If you look very closely, you will notice that the spline is not as thick as the segment. I have aligned it with the inside of the segment, not the outside. During the lathe-turning the segment wood at the corner intersections will be turned away, so there was no need to build the splines as thick as the segments.

This type of ring must be constructed perfectly round because just a slight oval shape will result in portholes that are not all the same depth. For that reason I like to add a matching-sized waste block when I glue the ring together. This allows me to confirm the roundness of the ring and to tweak the roundness slightly, if necessary, before the glue sets. If the miters are precise, very little tweaking should be necessary. I once again dry-assembled the ring of 14 pieces with attached splines, and turned a piece of 3/4-inch MDF to match its outside diameter.

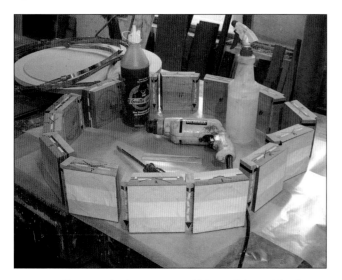

15-11   Be sure to have everything at hand before spreading any glue.

15-12   A waste block can be attached at the same time that the ring is glued.

15-13   A sharp cutting tool is essential.

I gathered everything that was needed (**photo 15-11**) and glued the ring together. To increase the open time, I used polyurethane (Gorilla) glue. In the photo, notice the water bottle: I sprayed a light mist over the joints before gluing. Polyurethane glue is moisture-activated and sets better with the presence of a little moisture. Four hose clamps provided clamping pressure and a pipe clamp from the ceiling held the waste block in place (**photo 15-12**). I took special care to align all the segment intersections and to center the MDF waste block.

After allowing the glue to cure overnight, I very carefully turned the ring on the lathe (**photo 15-13**). The porthole openings meant that my sharp bowl gouge was cutting air most of the time. To minimize chip-out at the porthole edges I took very light cuts at the highest reasonable lathe speed. The ring's inside surface was much easier to turn, although care had to be taken to maintain sufficient wall thickness behind the face designs. Far too much work had gone into the project to get careless at this stage — I checked frequently with a double-ended wall thickness caliper. Because of the porthole segments, this portion of the vessel had to have thicker walls than the top and bottom portions. This was unavoidable and not obvious from the outside; on the inside, the portholes do slightly interrupt the vessel curvature.

With the porthole ring done, I finalized my blueprint for the remainder of the vessel. I divided the construction into three different sections: the porthole ring with its two adjoining feature rings, the bottom section, and the upper section. I independently built each section and then combined them into the final vessel form. I am not going to describe every little detail regarding the rest of the project because I have discussed ring-building techniques in previous chapters, but I will detail a few noteworthy techniques.

15-14   The center portion of the vessel is composed of eleven layers.

15-15   A sabre saw can be used to split a large ring.

Large Diameter Ring Techniques

Broken Spirits is about 22 inches in diameter. I have built many larger vessels, but this is certainly large enough to demonstrate a few techniques. After completing the porthole ring I built the two smaller feature rings, which I positioned above and below the porthole ring. I used the disc sander extensively to fit the individual elements of these two rings. In addition, my design called for thin layers of wood above and below these two smaller feature rings. If you take a close look at the middle portion of the vessel, you can count five layers above and below the porthole ring. The technique used to join all these large rings was slightly different than for smaller rings. **Photo 15-14** displays the eleven layers, from left to right they are maple, jarrah, feature ring, jarrah, maple, porthole ring, maple, jarrah, feature ring, jarrah, and maple.

Here is how I assembled these layers together:

I had already attached the porthole ring to a faceplate during the previous glue job. Instead of gluing together the four thin maple and jarrah rings, I created two thicker rings of each

type of wood, which I could split into thinner rings. **Photo 15-15** shows one of the maple rings center-mounted on a circle of MDF with a continuous bead of hot-melt glue. I have turned the outside of the ring round and flattened its surface for gluing. I did not turn the interior curve of the ring, but left it alone with its segment corners. To split the ring, I used a thin parting tool from the outside surface. I did not cut all the way through the ring because it was too fragile — a slight bump could have broken it. If you look closely at the inside corners of the ring, you'll see where the parting tool barely broke through. A little uncut wood between the segment corners still holds the two ring-halves together. The small break-through slot created by the parting tool provided an entry point for a sabre saw blade, making it easy to separate the ring. I then put aside the cut-off thin ring with its one ready-to-glue surface.

I flattened the lathe-mounted half of the maple ring, then hot-glued a ring of jarrah to it (**photo 15-16**, next page). I used the same process shown in **photo 15-15** to flatten and then split the jarrah ring. I put aside the separated jarrah ring with its smooth surface and proceeded to flatten the lathe-mounted half.

15-16   Notice the small slots where the parting tool cut through at the glue joints.

15-17   Sanding blocks must be very straight and flat.

15-18   This is just one of many clamping steps.

Glue bead

15-19   Small beads of hot-melt glue can temporarily hold rings during flattening.

15-20   When spring clamps are too small, bar clamps can be used.

15-21   Notice the masking tape that protects the portholes from dripping glue.

Before I removed the second half-ring of jarrah I flattened it using a large sanding block with 80-grit paper attached (**photo 15-17**). It is critical that the mating glue surfaces be perfectly flat. A tiny inaccuracy on both surfaces can combine to create a detectable flaw in the seam. Make sure your sanding block is perfectly straight. As sanding-block sizes increase, flatness and straightness become even more critical.

I glued one of the thin jarrah rings to the lathe-mounted ring of maple using many spring clamps, as shown in **photo 15-18**.

I used hot-melt glue to temporarily attach one of the feature rings to the jarrah ring (**photo 15-19**). I turned it round, flattened a glue surface, removed it from the jarrah ring, flattened the jarrah ring, and glued the feature ring onto the assembly.

I added another maple ring and jarrah ring (the ones that had been set aside) to the feature ring.

The next layer is the porthole ring. I flattened the surface, matched the diameters, removed it from its waste block, and glued it to the assembly using bar clamps as in **photo 15-20**.

Using the waste block that I had removed from the porthole ring, I mounted the other full-sized maple ring, assembled the upper third of this section, and then added it to the upper surface of the porthole ring as shown in **photo 15-21**.

Building Sunrise Segments

I built two additional feature rings, one for the lower portion and one for the top portion of the vessel. The construction of these small sunrise depictions was a little different from disc-sander-built elements.

I first constructed half-round segmented rings using the previously discussed half-ring technique (Chapter 7). I disc-sanded the half-rings to form whole rings, but did not glue the halves together.

I dry-clamped the glued halves together with two unglued purpleheart splines separating them. **Photo 15-22** displays three of these rings. With the pairs of half-rings hose-clamped

15-22   This requires a drill press and a sharp forstner bit.

15-23   Check the fit as you turn.

together I drilled 1/2-inch holes in all the ring centers and inserted a piece of 1/2-inch dowel, as shown in the foreground ring.

The dowel provided a means of accurately centering a Forstner bit on the drill press, to create a larger, smooth-sided hole in the other rings. The two half-rings in the photo show the result of removing the hose clamp.

I needed to transform these rings into rectangular segments, but first I needed to fill the center holes. I used the half-rings with their half-holes as guide templates to turn plugs, as shown in **photo 15-23**. The turning had to be very accurate, any gap would be easily visible.

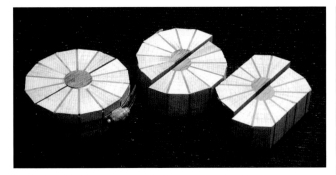

15-24   These steps eventually result in a segment.

15-25   Because of the vessel profile, this ring must be dimensioned quite thick.

15-26   Almost invisible glue lines are a result of maintaining grain orientation.

15-27   Follow the gluing steps clockwise, starting from the lower left.

To glue and clamp the cylinders, I used a hose clamp as shown on the left side of **photo 15-24**. I aligned the grain of the plug so that it would be horizontal in the vessel wall. Notice that the dry purpleheart splines are no longer separating the two halves. I separated the two half-rings with the band saw and smoothed the surface on the disc sander, as shown in the center of the photo. Then I used the table saw to make a parallel cut as shown on the right side of the photo. Using the miter saw I made miter cuts to transform these assemblies into ring segments. Next I cut narrow splines with horizontal grain to separate the segments. Two different sized rings were needed: one for the top portion and one for the bottom portion of the vessel. The larger of these two rings is shown in **photo 15-25** as it is prepared for stacking to the other layers.

Another Method of Inserting Diamonds

Other than building conventional rings of mesquite for the main body of the vessel, only one additional chore remains. Three of the mesquite rings have small Indian blanket diamonds embedded within the segments. These are much larger than the router-created diamonds shown in Chapter 11. I did not want any noticeable glue lines so I laminated these designs into the ring segments as follows:

First, I built the Indian blanket designs using the technique described in Chapter 9. I used the miter saw and disc sander to create the bordered diamond shapes shown in **photo 15-26**. This photo also shows a few blocks of mesquite, left and right sides of segments that I cut and

15-28   A straight edge can be used reveal a flat spot on the profile.

reassembled with the diamond design surrounded. I used the band saw to split the blocks horizontally, the red line (**photo 15-26**) represents this cut line. I numbered all the blocks so I could reassemble them in their original configuration, which would match the grain and hide the glue lines.

The next photo (**15-27**) shows the steps that I used to build the diamond-embedded segments. In the bottom left, an unassembled segment has four 45° miter cuts surrounding the diamond center. After checking the fit against a bright light and adjusting as necessary, I did the gluing in two steps: first one side as shown in the top left of the photo, then the second step as shown in the top right. After I achieved a perfect fit surrounding the diamonds, I cut the ends opposite the angled cuts flush with each other. During gluing I knew that if the ends were even, then the inside of the angle would be correctly aligned. When applying the clamp glue squeeze-out obscures the view of the inside miter corners, therefore aligning the trimmed ends is the best way to position them. In the bottom right, I show a completed block ready to be miter-cut into a ring segment.

More Large-Vessel Techniques

The remainder of the project consisted of assembling and stacking rings. I built the vessel from both the top and bottom directions and made the final glue line just below the center feature ring. Creating a smooth profile with a consistent wall thickness on such a large vessel

can be challenging. When turning smaller vessels, we usually finish the outside shape and then turn the inside to a consistent thickness. Because of the depth and limited access, when turning large and deep vessels I usually rough-turn both inside and outside surfaces as I stack the rings, and try to finish-turn the inside before I have to reach excessively. This can lead to problems if I do not frequently check diameters against my blueprint. If two different profiles (inside and outside) exist, then the wall thickness will not be consistent. For that reason I try to maintain as much wall thickness as possible for as long as possible, giving me maximum options during the final shaping. Large vessels tend to have very subtle curves, which can make it easy to unintentionally produce a flat spot on the profile. It is not always that easy to see and create the desired subtle curve. One trick, and this might sound a little funny, is to use a straight-edge on the curve. By placing a ruler against the vessel profile and rolling it from point to point, you can easily detect flat spots (**photo 15-28**). A straight line against a curved line should only make contact at one tiny spot at a time. If the ruler makes more than point contact anywhere along the vessel profile, you immediately know where a little more shaping is required.

With the bottom half completed, I prepared the upper half for its attachment (**photo 15-29**, next page). I completed as much of the finish work as possible, all that remained was the top rim of ebony, left thick to provide secure attachment to its waste block.

15-29   The top half is almost ready for the last gluing step.

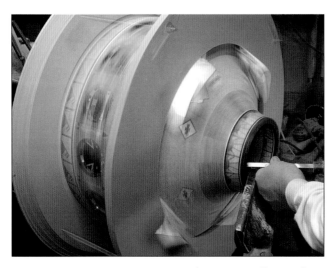

15-30   Reverse mounting at this stage allows the top to be finished.

15-31   A hand-held cabinet scraper and power sanding finishes the inside seam.

I knew from experience that once I assembled the two halves, the final shaping of the top rim would be difficult. Because of the height (30 inches) and relatively small base (less than 6 inches), without the aid of a tailstock or large steady-rest, the top would vibrate excessively. I avoided this by reverse-mounting the top half as shown in **photo 15-30**. The mounting technique used 1-inch MDF for the headstock side and 3/4-inch MDF for the donut-shaped retaining ring. Four lengths of all-thread rod held the turning in place, with thin rubber pads protecting its surface. To ensure perfect centering I turned a shallow groove into the 1-inch MDF, which held the vessel half in the correct position. I used a fairly slow lathe speed to finish the top shaping and sanding.

With matching inside and outside diameters, I joined the two halves. The base faceplate remained mounted on the vessel bottom. The cleanup of the last glue line required very little turning. I was able to clean up the inside seam with a curved handheld cabinet scraper, followed by power-sanding. The outside seam required a little shear-scraping followed by sanding. **Photo 15-31** shows my arm reaching into the vessel as I power-sand the inside seam with a 3-inch disc. You can see the power cord (under my arm) with a piece of masking tape on it, this is a sort of depth gauge indicating the approximate location of the sanding disc inside the vessel.

After multiple applications of oil finish, it was time to remove the base waste block and faceplate. Reverse-mounting the entire vessel without the aid of a tailstock was not an option, so I routed off most of the waste block, then used a 3-inch, drill-mounted sanding disc to finish the bottom. I would have preferred lathe-turning the base, but without a tailstock or large steady-rest, it was just too risky.

Large turnings such as *BROKEN SPIRITS* can be scary for several reasons. The rotational speed of large diameters can be intimidating, but perhaps the scariest aspect is the possibility of a serious mishap wiping out weeks of time and effort. The greater the risk, the greater the

15-32   *DECEPTION ON THE COCOBOLO* (42 inches tall) — large pieces require creative solutions.

reward. I enjoy the challenges of large turnings but I am always relieved when a project such as this is out of the studio.

Large turnings do not need to be vessel forms. Architectural forms and furniture items are also possibilities. One of my recent large projects, *DECEPTION ON THE COCOBOLO*, is shown in **photo 15-32**. The title was chosen because of the nature of the game of chess and for the cocobolo squares that compose part of the playing surface. The table top is 43 inches in diameter and for structural strength, the wall thickness of most components averages 3/4 inch. This project required more than segmented woodturning skills. The chairs swivel on bearings and the table top contains two hidden dovetailed drawers for storing the playing pieces, which are all segmented, lead-weighted, and leather-based. This project was treated as several different projects, which I tackled one at a time.

First I created the playing pieces, which are larger than official tournament size (5-1/2 inch king), then I built the chess board in proportion to the pieces. I researched the recommended proportion and found the little-known specification that the largest base diameter should be 78% of the square dimensions. The table top with its drawers was next, at which point I had to decide between bar-stool height or normal table height. After building the three pedestals, I finished the project by building the chair seats. As I jokingly tell people, this was not done in a weekend. It was, however, a very satisfying project that had been bouncing around in my head for a long time. It illustrates the idea that if you can think it, you can build it.

16-01   *TURBULENCE* (34 inches tall) — segments in motion.

16.
Segmented Ribbons

There seems to be no end to the number of segmented design possibilities. At first glance, most people would never guess that the form *TURBULENCE* (**photo 16-01**)was created on a lathe. It takes experienced woodturners a few moments to visualize the method of construction: each of the corners or changes in direction represents one half of a turned, bottomless bowl. *TURBULENCE* is nothing more than eight, stave-constructed bowls. The bowls were turned with identical diameters, wall thicknesses, and 45° slope angles. I then cut the eight bowls into sixteen half-bowls using a band saw. After using a disc sander to clean up the saw cuts, I reconnected the half-bowls end to end to create the twisting loop. This technique is not for the timid, many potential disasters lurk in the shadows. But for those who are interested, the following is a step-by-step description of a project using this technique.

As with most woodworking projects, it starts with a plan. Questions have to be answered:

• How many corners or half bowls are required?

• What diameter should the bowls be?

• What wood species to use and what (if any) is the desired pattern of segments?

For this project I am going to construct a loop consisting of six half-bowls. I decided to build the three bowls with about a 10-inch diameter, using 24 staves in each bowl. The exact dimensions were not important as long as all three bowls are identical. A quick calculation [(10 x 3.1416) ÷ 24] told me that the wide end of the staves should be about 1.3 inches. There was no need to draw a blueprint for the bowl construction, since I knew that the slope angle

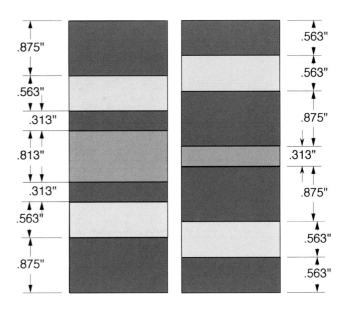

16-02   The layout of lamination layers should create a bricklay effect between staves.

had to be 45° and I knew the required width of the staves. I did, however, need to figure out the layout of the laminations from which to cut the staves. Each stave was cut from a seven-layer lamination, but these laminations were glued end-grain to end-grain, unlike most laminations. This was necessary so that when the staves were cut from the lamination, they could be glued together side-grain to side-grain. Side-grain glue joints are much stronger and more dependable. With this design, for the short end-grain glue joints within the staves to overlap, two different laminations were needed. **Photo 16-02** shows these particular layouts.

The boards that I selected were only about 5-1/2 inches wide. Therefore, the laminations from which I cut the staves could not be longer than about 5-1/2 inches. After a little arithmetic, I determined that I could cut five staves from each 5-1/2 inch long lamination. Three bowls with 24 staves per bowl meant that I needed 72 staves. To be on the safe side, I glued together 16 laminations, resulting in a yield of 80 staves. To produce the individual lamination components, I cross-cut the required pieces from three different types of wood (Texas ebony, maple, and eucalyptus). To insure extremely consistent widths and very smooth gluing surfaces, I

16-03   The accuracy and smoothness of the components is essential.

16-04   To accurately cut staves, the laminations must be smooth and consistent.

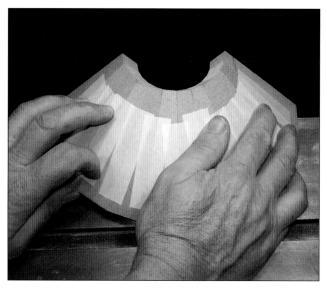

16-05   Test fitting and adjusting saw settings can take some time.

attached these strips to particleboard trays using double-sided tape and passed them through a drum sander. **Photo 11-12** in Chapter 11 shows a similar procedure. This might seem like over-kill, but I wanted the very best joints and I wanted the overall widths of the finished laminations to be very consistent. Each small lamination consisted of seven layers of end-grain to end-grain. End-grain joints will soak-up lots of glue, so I made sure to apply plenty of glue to both surfaces of each joint. The cut-offs are shown in **photo 16-03** before being glued and the completed laminations are shown in **photo 16-04**. To clean up the laminations, I handheld one side against a disc sander and then passed them through the drum sander using 36-grit paper.

The next step was to cut the compound miters from these laminations. The required angles are listed in the compound miter chart in the appendix. It is a simple matter of looking up 24 staves with a 45° slope angle in the chart. The specified blade angle is 5.3° and the miter is 84.68°. Because the width of the laminations was short, I decided to cut the staves on my sliding-compound miter saw; I could have just as easily used a sled on my table saw. There are two goals: to produce tight-fitting glue joints between the staves, and to produce a 45° slope angle on the bowl sides. The 45° angle is critical to success. There is a little extra thickness to play with during the shaping of the bowl on the lathe, but I recommend trying to achieve a slope angle as close as possible to 45° during the assembly of staves. There are 48 miter angles (two for each stave), so the opportunity for cumulative errors is great. To dial in my saw settings, I made a series of trial cuts from 3/4-inch MDF. After cutting 12 staves, I taped them together and rolled them into a half-bowl shape. Then I used the 90° angle between my disc sander table and disc to check the fit. After three attempts with slight saw adjustments, I was able to hold the 12 taped staves against the disc and confirm that I was very close to my goal. In **photo 16-05**, I am checking this fit. The seams have to be tight and the ends of the assembly have to fit flush against the disc. At this point, I could have cut another 12 staves and formed a complete cone shape to further confirm my saw settings, but I was confident that it was close enough, so I proceeded to cut the good stuff. **Photo 16-06** shows the miter saw set-up that I used.

Notice the MDF compound-mitered stop block. This is different from a typical pointed or flat stop block. It was cut with the same angle as the staves. The advantage of this stop block is that as my lamination is cut shorter, it becomes impossible to position it properly against the back fence. As you can see in the photo, the lamination has more contact with the stop block than it does with the back fence. I can rely upon this style of stop block for the needed support and angle. It does, however, require extra care in keeping the saw-bed clean of debris, which would otherwise become trapped between the lamination and the stop block.

It is tempting to glue the staves together without sanding the gluing surfaces. This might be OK with many of the joints, but it only takes one imperfect seam to ruin the entire project, so sand the stave sides. The staves were at the desired angle, so only a smidgen of material needed to be removed. If your sanding disc has seen a lot of use, then this would be a good time to install fresh paper. To adjust the sanding table to the correct angle, I test-sanded several pieces with pencil marks along the top and bottom edges (the edges closest to the inside and outside of the staves). When I could lightly touch a stave to the spinning disc and remove equal amounts off the pencil marks, I knew that I was not significantly changing the stave angles. It takes a very light touch to remove imperfections left by the saw blade. I used a bright light to inspect each surface before gluing. **Photo 16-07** shows a stave being lightly sanded.

A multi-step gluing process is needed to complete the cones. Because of the 45° slope angle, a gluing jig as shown in Chapter 11 will not work. **Photo 16-08** shows the first two steps. To accomplish steps three and four (photos on next page) I used a combination of duct tape and rubber bands. Using duct tape as a

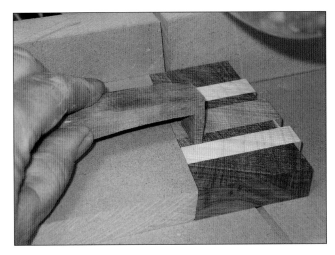

16-06   The compound-mitered stop block provides stability and accuracy.

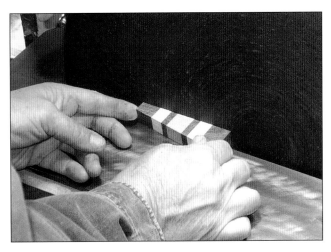

16-07   Think of the disc sander as a big eraser that gently removes imperfections.

16-08   Gluing the staves together is a multi-step process.

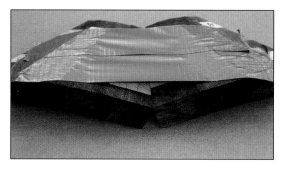

16-09   If applied correctly, duct tape can be used as a clamp.

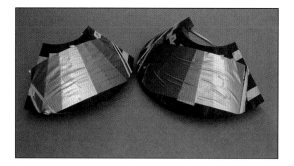

16-10   These are awkward shapes to clamp.

16-11   The last gluing step uses rubber bands anchored by little hot-glued blocks of MDF.

clamping aid requires a little practice. The attached tape in **photo 16-09** is stretched across the glue joint so that when the joint is closed, the tape will become even more stretched (**photo 16-10**). The tape's elasticity applies pressure to the outside of the joint. Rubber bands are then used to close the inside of the joint. The key to success is to have near-equal pressure applied to both sides of the seam. After trying this a few times dry, you should be able to use this clamping method effectively. Of course without a perfect fit between the staves, it matters little what type of clamping method you use.

Before gluing together the groups of 8 and 12 staves, I assembled them dry and checked the accuracy. The half-cone shapes had to be near perfect, an oval shape would likely require too much removal of material to create a round shape. A little disc-sander touch-up early in the assembly process can avoid the need for a major adjustment towards the end. Before gluing the completed halves together, one last touch-up on the disc sander was required. The simplest clamping method for this shape and size is,

once again, rubber bands. To prevent the bands from slipping on the cone, I attached a few pieces of scrap MDF with hot melt glue. **Photo 16-11** shows a completed glue job.

It's finally time to do some turning. After flattening the large ends of the cones on the disc sander, I mounted them to a large waste block with a few beads of hot-melt glue. This allowed me to rough-turn the outside and to turn a flat spot on the small end, to which I glued a small disc of 3/4-inch MDF. Once this connection cured, I turned the MDF disc so it could be used in a four-jaw chuck (**photo 16-12**). There was only a small amount of gluing surface holding the MDF disc on the cones, so I avoided any aggressive turning.

With the cones now mounted with their small ends toward the chuck, my first goal was to turn the outside of each to a 45° slope. After a little rough turning, I determined which of the three cones had the smallest outside diameter and then turned the other two cones to match. To determine the slope angle, I used a 45° square in conjunction with a straight ruler. **Photo 16-13** shows my square and straight edge as I checked the angle. Accuracy was critical, if one bowl is 43° and another is 47°, the total error will be 4° and a continuous loop will not be possible. Along with checking the slope angle, the outside diameters must be checked and adjusted to be equal. The rim of the bowl should be turned square to the slope angle. Keeping the rim square makes it easier to measure the diameter. After confirming the diameters and slope angles, the sharp edges can then be rounded. To achieve consistency, it is likely that a bowl will have to be remounted, and perhaps more than once. Notice in **photo 16-13** the red X on the MDF disc, this is so I can re-chuck the bowl with the same jaw orientation. Also notice that the MDF disc does not bottom out inside the chuck. It is supported on the face of the jaws. This is just one more little trick to increase stability. The more accurate you are at this stage, the easier it will be to reconnect the half-bowls later.

Turning the inside surfaces required creating a consistent wall thickness of about 1/4 inch. A thinner wall was certainly possible and perhaps more esthetically pleasing, but I was uncomfortable about sacrificing strength. The same 45° square/ruler technique can be used to check the inner surface. If the wall thickness at the rim is 1/4 inch and both inside and outside slope angles are 45°, then in theory, the wall thickness should be consistent. However, I still recommend checking it with a thickness gauge.

I power-sanded all the accessible surfaces and then reverse mounted the cones on a piece of MDF. To ensure centering, I turned a recessed groove into a large MDF waste block to accept the large end of the cones and used a donut-shaped retaining ring to secure them for the finish turning of the small ends (**photo 16-14**). After a little more turning and sanding, the cones were ready to be cut apart.

As segmented turners, we rarely have an opportunity to easily repair a defective glue line. This is one of those rare opportunities: if a seam between the staves is discovered to be less than perfect, it can be corrected by choosing that seam as the location for the band-saw cut.

16-12   This waste block is ready to be mounted in a four-jaw chuck.

16-13   A straight edge and 45° square are used to check the slope angle.

16-14   Attach the retaining ring, turn the donut ring, and then secure the cone shape.

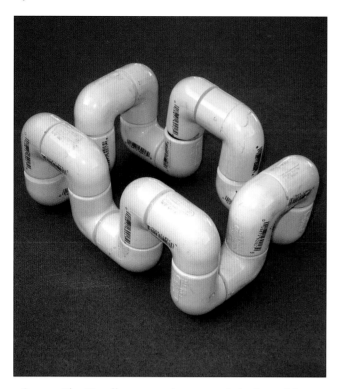

16-15   Plastic elbows make a great design aid.

16-16   This method requires equal pressure on both sides of the glue joint.

When cutting the bowls apart, avoid the mistake of messing up the pattern. To understand what I mean, look at the center strip of pink wood in **photo 16-14**. The segments alternate from large to small. The bowls must be cut so that the pattern continues with the new alignment, otherwise when reassembled two segments of the same size will be positioned next to each other. Compared to *TURBULENCE* (page 166), this is a simple shape to assemble. When constructing more complicated forms, it helps to have a model to visualize. Many different shapes can be constructed using 90° plastic plumbing elbows. **Photo 16-15** shows a possible shape that could be built using half-bowl shapes. A model can certainly help you avoid a major glue-joint direction error.

After careful cutting on the band saw and a little touch-up on the disc sander, the half-bowls were ready to be joined. Clamping such odd-shaped pieces together can be a challenge. My solution uses a combination of small blocks of scrap wood, hot-melt glue, and rubber bands. If you study **photo 16-16**, you will quickly understand the technique. A key to success is to

apply equal pressure on both sides of the glue joints with the bands. Alignment of the ends, of course, is also important. The goal is to minimize sanding after the glue has cured, which will also help hide the transition between sections. I divided the gluing into three steps. First, I joined the two sets of halves which comprise the horizontal curves. After sanding these joints, I connected them with a vertical section at each end. To make sure that everything would come together on the final joint, I first dry clamped both ends. Then I unclamped one end, applied the glue, and put it back together. Once this seam had cured, I glued the final seam together. While applying the rubber bands, you will wish you had another pair of hands, so if possible enlist a friend.

The sanding of the seams was relatively easy using 3-inch power-sanding discs, although the inside corners did require a little handwork. All in all, this is not a difficult project, but it does require a multitude of woodworking and woodturning skills. Perhaps the most fun is hearing people say, "How did he do that?"

16-17   *CHAPTER 16* (10 in. x 10 in. x 16 in.) — Now you know how to do that.

The last and certainly not the least important task was to name the piece — titles are important. They provide a verbal handle for people when they refer to your work, and they can help tell a story or convey a message. This particular piece was a rush job in order to include this technique in the book. So what better name than ... *Chapter 16* (**photo 16-17**). This technique opens the door to many other possibilities. Instead of half-bowls, quarter and/or three-quarter bowl shapes could be used. Instead of bowls, donut-shaped components could be used. There is no end to where our imaginations can take us.

17-01   *HEARTS OF LIGHT* (36 inches tall) — 6,500 individual pieces of wood and a lot of careful planning.

17.
Final Thoughts

People that meet me after viewing my work often remark that I must be very patient. I have never thought of myself as a patient person, quite the contrary. Progress on turning projects always seems too slow. There is always a feeling of urgency to finish a turning once I have started, but I have learned to be methodical in my approach, so perhaps I have become a more patient person because of my experiences. I have certainly learned that it does not pay to rush a project. Hurrying results in mistakes and possibly accidents and actually slows down progress. One of the most asked questions is, "How long did it take you to make that?" I sometimes reply, "Does it matter?" We all have to eat, but there is a difference between turning to live and living to turn. *HEARTS OF LIGHT* (**photo 17.01**), with its more than 6000 individual pieces of wood, certainly requires one to be passionate about the art and perhaps less concerned about the time required or the financial bottom line.

There is an old saying that the best woodworker is the one who best hides his mistakes. In segmented turning construction, there are very few opportunities to hide mistakes. All the glue joints and every square millimeter of surface are subject to close scrutiny. The intricacy of segmented work almost begs people to closely examine it. People sometimes even seem challenged to discover a flaw. The most exacting assembly techniques in the field of woodworking are required and compromises usually lead to disappointment. The late Ray Allen used to challenge people to find a loose joint in his turnings, he was very proud of his work for he knew that imperfections did not exist. He was absolutely right about the need for perfect joints, no matter how large or complex, no matter how beautiful the wood, a turning will lose much of its appeal if a viewer detects less than perfection in its construction. To help

you achieve perfection, and to help ensure that your turnings stay together for a very long time, keep these things in mind:

- Use only dry wood (under 10% moisture content).

- Avoid intersections longer than 1 inch of opposing wood grain orientation (shorter if possible).

- Always consider the shape as the most important design element (more important than wood type, color combinations, etc).

- Never glue two surfaces together that do not fit perfectly and remember, a sanded joint will usually be stronger and have a better appearance.

- Do not resort to filling a joint imperfection. Re-do or replace as necessary. The defect will almost always show and you will inevitably regret the lack of perfection later.

- Avoid an abundance of oily wood to oily wood glue lines.

- Keep, and inform others to keep your turnings away from excessive exposure to direct sunlight (the colors will fade).

Everything evolves, and woodturning art is no exception. It was not that long ago, when the cover of *Fine WoodWorking* magazine displayed two segmented vessels by Addie Draper and Bud Latven. I dusted off that old issue recently and could not help but compare their magnificent 1985 work to a recent AAW Instant Gallery display of member's work — evolution is alive and well. Learning and discovering are big reasons why this art form is so enjoyable. Solving the puzzles of new design challenges keeps your brain active and rewards you with fantastic feelings of satisfaction. To quote a line from an old Bob Dylan song, "He not busy being born is busy dying." I feel my own journey of discovery has just begun, endless possibilities keep me intrigued. Good luck with your own journey! I hope my efforts with this book have provided you with a foundation and that your own discoveries will contribute to the advancement of this wonderful art form.

Appendix

Mathematical Formulas and Concepts

A circle contains 360°

Circumference equals diameter multiplied by pi (3.1416)

Diameter equals circumference divided by pi (3.1416)

Segment length equals circumferences divided by number of segments

Segment angle equals 360° divided by number of segments divided by 2

Calculating Compound Miters:

Miter Angle (MA)
$$= \text{inverse tan} \ (1 \div [\cos S * \tan(360 \div 2N)])$$

Blade Angle (BA)
$$= \text{inverse tan} \ (\cos MA * \tan S)$$

MA is the miter angle

S is the slope of the vessel (measured from horizontal to side)

BA is the saw blade angle (the bevel cut)

N is the number of staves

Construction of Platonic Solids:

Shape	Miter Angle*
Tetrahedron	54.735°
Hexahedron (cube)	45.000°
Octahedron	35.264°
Icosahedron	20.905°
Dodecahedron	31.717°

* This is the edge miter of the individual components as listed in Magnus Wenninger's book, *Spherical Models*.

Compound Miter Angles for Stave-Constructed Forms

	6 Staves		8 Staves	
Slope*	Miter Angle	Blade Angle	Miter Angle	Blade Angle
0	60.00	0.00	67.50	0.00
5	60.09	2.50	67.58	1.91
10	60.38	4.98	67.81	3.81
15	60.85	7.44	68.19	5.68
20	61.52	9.85	68.73	7.52
25	62.38	12.20	69.42	9.31
30	63.43	14.48	70.27	11.03
35	64.69	16.67	71.26	12.68
40	66.14	18.75	72.40	14.24
45	67.79	20.70	73.68	15.70
50	69.64	22.52	75.09	17.05
55	71.68	24.18	76.64	18.27
60	73.90	25.66	78.30	19.35
65	76.29	26.95	80.07	20.29
70	78.83	28.02	81.94	21.08
75	81.50	28.88	83.88	21.69
80	84.27	29.50	85.89	22.14
85	87.12	29.87	87.93	22.41
90	90.00	30.00	90.00	22.50

* Slope is the angle from the horizontal surface to the vertical side assuming that the form is positioned with the small end pointed down.

Compound Miter Angles
for Stave-Constructed Forms

Slope*	10 Staves Miter Angle	10 Staves Blade Angle	12 Staves Miter Angle	12 Staves Blade Angle	16 Staves Miter Angle	16 Staves Blade Angle	20 Staves Miter Angle	20 Staves Blade Angle	24 Staves Miter Angle	24 Staves Blade Angle
0	72.00	0.00	75.00	0.00	78.75	0.00	81.00	0.00	82.50	0.00
5	72.06	1.54	75.05	1.29	78.79	0.97	81.03	0.78	82.53	0.65
10	72.26	3.08	75.22	2.58	78.92	1.94	81.13	1.56	82.61	1.30
15	72.58	4.59	5.49	3.84	79.12	2.89	81.30	2.32	82.75	1.94
20	73.02	6.07	75.87	5.08	79.41	3.83	81.53	3.07	82.95	2.56
25	73.59	7.50	76.35	6.28	79.78	4.73	81.83	3.79	83.20	3.16
30	74.28	8.89	76.94	7.44	80.23	5.60	82.19	4.49	83.50	3.74
35	75.10	10.21	77.62	8.54	80.75	6.42	82.61	5.15	83.84	4.29
40	76.02	11.46	78.40	9.58	81.34	7.20	83.08	5.77	84.24	4.81
45	77.06	12.62	79.27	10.55	81.99	7.93	83.61	6.35	84.68	5.30
50	78.20	13.69	80.23	11.44	82.71	8.59	84.19	6.88	85.16	5.74
55	79.44	14.66	81.26	12.24	83.49	9.20	84.81	7.36	85.68	6.14
60	80.77	15.52	82.37	12.95	84.32	9.73	85.47	7.79	86.23	6.49
65	82.18	16.26	83.54	13.57	85.19	10.18	86.17	8.15	86.82	6.79
70	83.66	16.88	84.76	14.08	86.11	10.56	86.90	8.45	87.42	7.05
75	85.19	17.37	86.03	14.48	87.05	10.86	87.65	8.69	88.05	7.24
80	86.77	17.72	87.34	14.77	88.02	11.08	88.42	8.86	88.69	7.39
85	88.38	17.93	88.66	14.94	89.01	11.21	89.21	8.97	89.34	7.47
90	90.00	18.00	90.00	15.00	90.00	11.25	90.00	9.00	90.00	7.50

* Slope is the angle from the horizontal surface to the vertical side assuming that the form is positioned with the small end pointed down.

Description of Turnings

11-26
p. 113
TEACUP FOR ALICE
4" tall
—laminated stave construction, offset mounted.
—purpleheart, holly, ebony, diamond wood (handle).

11-27
p. 113
CURVES
29" tall
—construction used laminated segments with angled orientation
—curly maple, pau ferro, ebony, diamond wood.

11-40
p. 117
FOR GAUDI
18" tall
—router created diamonds.
—individually turned staves.
—canarywood, pau ferro, holly, ebony, rosewood.

11-49
p. 121
BLACKBERRY SWIRL
6.5" tall
—made from angled rings cut from a single ring.
—purpleheart, holly, ebony.

12-01
p. 122
QUILTED BOWLS
5.5" tall
—brick-laid segments, 901 pieces each.
—curly maple, ebony, rosewood, purpleheart, yellowheart, jarrah, bloodwood, mesquite.

13-06
p. 128
OVAL BOWL #9L
5" tall
—created by cutting a bowl shape in half and rejoining.
—mesquite, ebony, yellowheart, rosewood, pink ivory.

13-07
p. 131
ROCK 'N ROLLER
16" diameter donuts
—almost 2000 individual pieces.
—bubinga, maple, and many exotics.

13-14
p. 134
INTEGRATION
12" diameter donuts.
—walnut and curly maple.

13-15
p. 135
GROWTH
27" tall
—mitered rings, screwed together.
—myrtlewood and ebony.

13-16
p. 135
TALKING WITH WOOD
8.5" tall
—over 1500 pieces of wood.
—holly, ebony, carob, mesquite, bloodwood, yellowheart, purpleheart, jarrah, maple, pink ivory.

14-04
p. 138
COSMOS with **SATELLITE BOXES**
36" tall
—icosahedron style sphere surrounded by free spinning rings.
—many exotics.

14-01
p. 139
ANDY'S TOY
9" diameter
—an unturned icosahedron.
—pine and paint.

14-03
p. 139
THE JUGGLER
34" tall
—icosahedron style sphere, multi-lamination container at top.
—curly maple, ebony, and many exotics.

14-18
p. 146
PLATONIC MOLECULE
28" tall
—icosahedron style sphere with attached smaller spheres.
—jarrah, ebony, Bird's-eye maple, purpleheart, canarywood, bloodwood, tulipwood, cocobolo, black walnut.

14-24
p. 149
FOR JOHN GLENN
14" diameter
—sphere transformed into vessel.
—ironwood, tulipwood, ebony, other exotics.

14-25
p. 150
24 HOUR PITCHER
20" tall
—sphere transformed into vessel form.
—curly maple, ebony, and many exotics.

14-26
p. 150
MIDNIGHT SNOW
17" tall
—sphere with plug decorations transformed into vessel form.
—ebony, holly, curly maple.

14-27
p. 151
SPORTS BOWLS
life size
—many exotics.

15-00
p. 152
front
cover

BROKEN SPIRITS
30" tall
—more than 3000 individual pieces of wood.
—unique porthole construction as described in Chapter 15.
—Argentinean mesquite, curly maple, ebony, jarrah, purpleheart, pink ivory, holly, tulipwood, flamewood, bloodwood, canarywood, pau ferro, black walnut.

15-32
p. 165

DECEPTION ON THE COCOBOLO
43" diameter table top
—swivel seats, hidden storage drawers, segmented playing pieces.
—myrtlewood, walnut, curly maple, bloodwood, cocobolo, Bird's-eye maple, wenge, ebony, yellowheart.

16-01
p. 166

TURBULENCE
34" tall
—16 half-bowls reassembled into a twisted, segmented ribbon.
—many exotics.

16-17
p. 173

CHAPTER 16
10" x 10" x 16"
—6 half-bowls reassembled into a twisted, segmented ribbon.
—Texas ebony, maple, eucalyptus.

17-01
p. 174

HEARTS OF LIGHTS
36" tall
—router created heart shaped portholes.
—many exotics.

Bibliography

Brown, Emmett E. and Brown, Cyril, *Polychromatic Assembly for Woodturning,* Linden Publishing Co., 1982
Originally published by the Society of Ornamental Turners, England

Constantine, Jr., Albert, *Know Your Woods,* Macmillan Publishing Company, First Scribner Paperback Edition, 1987

Cox, Jack, *Beyond Basic Turning,* Linden Publishing, 1993

Daper, Addie and Latven, Bud, *Segmented Turning, Redefining an Old Technique,* Taunton Press, Inc, *Fine Woodworking* Magazine, September/October 1985, pages 64-67

Hoadley, R. Bruce, *Understanding Wood,* Taunton Press, Inc, 1980

Lincoln, William A., *World Woods in Color,* Linden Publishing, 1986

Nish, Dale L., *Artistic Woodturning,* Brigham Young University Press, 1980

Nish, Dale L., *Creative Woodturning,* Brigham Young University Press, 1975

Rannefeld, Clarence, *Laminated Designs in Wood,* Lark Books, 1998

Shuler, Michael, *Segmented Turning, Swirling patterns by cutting and reassembling a single board,* Taunton Press, Inc, *Fine Woodworking* Magazine, May/June, 1989, pages 72-75

Smith, William, *Segmented Turning,* Schiffer Publishing Ltd., 2002

Springett, David, *Woodturning Wizardry,* Guild of Master Craftsman Publications Ltd, 1993

Wenninger, Magnus, *Polyhedron Models,* Cambridge University Press, 1971

Wenninger, Magnus, *Spherical Models,* Dover Publications, Inc., 1999
        Originally published: Cambridge [Eng.] University Press, 1979

About the Author

Malcolm Tibbetts is a professional segmented woodturner living with his wife Tere in South Lake Tahoe, California. After raising two children and after more than thirty years as an executive in the ski industry, he now creates lathe-turned art objects fulltime for several galleries. His appreciation and experiences with wood assembly span fifty years going back to the days spent in his grandfather's shop as a youngster. His innovative work resides in prestigious collections throughout the world and his work has received many woodturning awards. As a member of the AAW (American Association of Woodturners) his contact information is publicly listed in the AAW Resource Directory. Feel free to contact him with your comments or questions through his website, www.tahoeturner.com.

Index